Cooking Basics

maranGraphics™

&

THOMSON

COURSE TECHNOLOGY

Professional ■ Technical ■ Reference

maranGraphics™

maranGraphics Inc.
5755 Coopers Avenue
Mississauga, Ontario
L4Z 1R9
www.maran.com

THOMSON

COURSE TECHNOLOGY

Professional ■ Technical ■ Reference

Thomson Course Technology PTR, a division of Thomson Course Technology
25 Thomson Place ■ Boston, MA 02210 ■ http://www.courseptr.com

maranGraphics is a family-run business

At **maranGraphics**, we believe in producing great books—one book at a time.

Each maranGraphics book uses the award-winning communication process that we have been developing over the last 30 years. Using this process, we organize photographs and text in a way that makes it easy for you to learn new concepts and tasks.

We spend hours deciding the best way to perform each task, so you don't have to! Our clear, easy-to-follow photographs and instructions walk you through each task from beginning to end.

We want to thank you for purchasing what we feel are the best books money can buy. We hope you enjoy using this book as much as we enjoyed creating it!

Sincerely,

The Maran Family

We would love to hear from you!
Send your comments and feedback about our books to family@maran.com

To sign up for sneak peeks and news about our upcoming books, send an e-mail to newbooks@maran.com

Please visit us on the Web at:
www.maran.com

CREDITS

Author:
maranGraphics
Development Group

Content Architects:
Kelleigh Johnson
Andrew Wheeler
Wanda Lawrie

**Technical Consultant,
Recipe Development & Testing:**
Gail Gordon Oliver

Editor & Recipe Testing:
Jill Maran Dutfield

Project Manager & Editor:
Judy Maran-Tarnowski

Copy Developers:
Kelleigh Johnson
Andrew Wheeler
Cathy Lo
Raquel Scott

Editor:
Ruth Maran

**Photographer, Layout Designer
& Photographic Retouching:**
Sarah Kim

**Layout Designer &
Photographic Retouching:**
Mark Porter

Nutrient Analysis:
Prepared by Heidi Smith, RD using
The Food Processor SQL, ESHA Research
www.heidismithnutrition.com

Post Production & Photography:
Robert Maran

**Publisher and General Manager,
Thomson Course Technology PTR:**
Stacy L. Hiquet

**Associate Director of Marketing,
Thomson Course Technology PTR:**
Sarah O'Donnell

**Manager of Editorial Services,
Thomson Course Technology PTR:**
Heather Talbot

ACKNOWLEDGMENTS

Thanks to the dedicated staff of maranGraphics, including
Kelleigh Johnson, Sarah Kim, Jill Maran Dutfield, Judy Maran-Tarnowski,
Robert Maran, Ruth Maran, Mark Porter and Andrew Wheeler.

Finally, to Richard Maran who originated the easy-to-use graphic
format of this guide. Thank you for your inspiration and guidance.

ABOUT THE TECHNICAL CONSULTANT...

Gail Gordon Oliver is a native of Montreal and attributes much of her passion for food and cooking to having grown up experiencing the gastronomic riches of her hometown. A graduate of McGill University, Gail embarked on her culinary career after moving to Toronto in 1996. As a student in the Culinary Management program at The George Brown Chef School, she received full chef and baking training. Following graduation, Gail worked in the highly regarded test kitchen of Canadian Living, a national magazine.

Gail is the owner of Flavours of Home (www.flavoursofhome.com), a Toronto-based culinary consulting company and cooking school. In addition to her freelance work in food writing, editing, recipe development and testing, Gail provides hands-on personalized culinary instruction tailored to the requirements of each client. Her cooking school offers a comprehensive learning program for the home cook.

A few words from Gail:

Many thanks to the Maran family for giving me the opportunity to provide the home cook with the terminology, skills and techniques used in professional kitchens. Combined with a unique layout, this book is sure to be used extensively as a reference guide. Thanks to talented writers Wanda, Kelleigh and Andrew, and artists Sarah and Mark, with whom I worked closely and who had to deal daily with my perfectionist tendencies.

I'd like to pay tribute to two special women who played a role in my culinary development. Much of my inspiration comes from fond food-related memories of my dear mother, Phyllis Chodos Gordon, and grandmother, Debbie Chodos, both deeply missed at this time.

Finally, to my wonderful husband Steven Oliver, and my incredible daughters, Amanda and Jillian: Your love, support and patience while I worked long days, nights and weekends on this book were unwavering. And, as my guinea pigs, thank you for being so accommodating when I served dinner well beyond "dinnertime" while creating recipes. As my official taste testers, many recipes in this book were perfected based on your valued feedback.

SPECIAL THANKS TO...

PADERNO
Pots for Eternity

A special thanks to Paderno for supplying the majority of the bakeware, cookware and kitchen tools featured in this book.

Paderno started in Prince Edward Island, Canada in 1979 with a vision of making cookware so good it would outlast anything else in the kitchen. Since those early beginnings, Paderno's superb quality pots and pans with an exceptional 25-year warranty have become famous across North America. That vision of excellent performance and outstanding durability has also helped Paderno develop an ever-widening range of kitchen products that continue to meet that standard.

For more information on Paderno's line of products call 1-800-A-NEW-POT or visit www.paderno.com.

ZWILLING J.A.HENCKELS

A special thanks to ZWILLING J.A. HENCKELS for supplying the knives used in this book.

ZWILLING J.A. HENCKELS still prides itself on making the finest cutlery available on the market. Today, the standards developed 275 years ago are still reflected in each piece that carries the ZWILLING J.A. HENCKELS name. The assortment has expanded from cutlery to include a wide variety of cooking-related products to meet the demands of today's consumer, including cookware, kitchen gadgets, tableware and scissors.

www.jahenckels.com (USA) or www.zwilling.com (Canada)

1-800-777-4308 (USA) or 905-475-2555 (Canada)

info@jahenckels.com (USA) or info@jahenckels.ca (Canada)

A special thanks to KitchenAid Home Appliances for supplying the majority of the appliances featured in this book. Certain KitchenAid photographs courtesy of KitchenAid Home Appliances.

KitchenAid®
FOR THE WAY IT'S MADE.™

Since the introduction of its legendary stand mixer in 1919 and first dishwasher in 1949, KitchenAid has built on the legacy of these icons to create a complete line of products designed for cooks. From countertop appliances to cookware, ranges to refrigerators, and whisks to wine cellars, KitchenAid now offers virtually every essential for the well-equipped kitchen. To view the entire KitchenAid line of appliances, visit www.KitchenAid.com.

A special thanks to Heidi Smith, RD, who provided the nutrient analysis for all of the recipes in this book using The Food Processor SQL by ESHA Research. For more information on Ms. Smith's services, visit www.heidismithnutrition.com.

A special thanks to Pyrex glassware for allowing their products to be used in this book. For more information about Pyrex® glassware, call 1-800-999-3436 or visit www.pyrexware.com.

Table of Contents

Table of Contents

Getting Started

For the beginner chef, the kitchen may seem like an intimidating place. This section will keep you from feeling overwhelmed by offering a thorough introduction to the basic kitchen tools, cookware, bakeware and appliances you will need. Also included in this section are helpful ideas on how to stock your kitchen and pantry as well as what to look for when you are at the grocery store.

Kitchen Tools

Stocking up on some basic kitchen tools can help make cooking easier and more enjoyable. The right tools can even help you become a more efficient cook, cutting down on the amount of time you need to spend in the kitchen.

CUTTING BOARDS

A well equipped kitchen should contain a selection of cutting boards, each for use with a different type of food. One cutting board should be used exclusively for cutting vegetables, another for fruit and a third for raw meat.

Cutting boards are available in wood, plastic and disposable plastic.

MIXING BOWLS

You will find your mixing bowls to be among the most indispensable items in your kitchen, used for mixing, whisking and assembling ingredients. As such, you should consider investing in stainless steel mixing bowls in a variety of sizes. Stainless steel bowls are lightweight, durable and easy to clean. They are also non-porous, making them more hygienic than other materials.

Colander

Strainers

COLANDER & STRAINERS

Colanders and strainers allow you to drain ingredients. You should have a large stainless steel colander for draining foods such as pasta, a medium-sized fine mesh strainer for draining items such as canned beans, and a small 2-inch diameter fine mesh strainer for straining smaller quantities of foods such as capers.

SALAD SPINNER

This handy tool removes water from freshly washed greens and herbs, preventing water-logged salads and delaying spoilage of greens.

VEGETABLE PEELER

You will need at least one vegetable peeler in your kitchen. Vegetable peelers have a stainless steel peeling mechanism and are available in a variety of handle types.

1-cup   2-cup   4-cup

LIQUID MEASURING CUPS

Liquid measuring cups allow you to measure wet ingredients such as milk or water. While liquid measuring cups are available in glass, plastic and metal, glass is recommended for ease of use and for getting an accurate reading. You should have at least one 1-cup, two 2-cup and one 4-cup liquid measuring cups.

DRY MEASURING CUPS

You should have at least one set of dry measuring cups for measuring ingredients such as flour and sugar. You can find a stacking set of dry measuring cups with 1/4-cup, 1/3-cup, 1/2-cup and 1-cup measures.

Dry measuring cups are also handy for measuring ingredients such as peanut butter, which are difficult to measure in a liquid measuring cup.

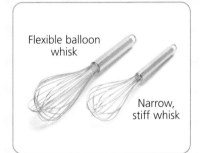

Flexible balloon whisk

Narrow, stiff whisk

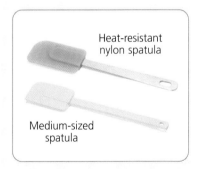

Heat-resistant nylon spatula

Medium-sized spatula

MEASURING SPOONS

Your kitchen would not be complete without a set of measuring spoons. These spoons are useful for measuring spices and baking ingredients such as baking powder and vanilla. Measuring spoons come in sets that include 1/8-teaspoon (tsp), 1/4-teaspoon, 1/2-teaspoon, 1-teaspoon and 1-tablespoon (tbsp) measures.

WHISKS

These versatile tools can be used for mixing dry ingredients, blending wet ingredients, and for whipping and beating. You should have at least two whisks that are between 8 and 10 inches long. Use a round flexible balloon whisk for beating air into ingredients such as whipping cream and a narrow, stiff whisk for soups, sauces and salad dressings.

RUBBER SPATULAS

Essential for baking, these spatulas are traditionally made of rubber but can be found in silicone versions as well. You should have at least one medium-sized rubber spatula for scraping batters from mixing bowls and at least one heat-resistant nylon or silicone spatula for stirring warm items such as custards.

PASTRY BRUSH

Whether you're baking or grilling, you'll find that pastry brushes come in handy. A natural bristles brush is best for applying glazes to breads and cakes. Silicone brushes are useful for adding seasoning to meats, poultry and fish.

MEAT POUNDER AND TENDERIZER

This useful tool does double duty, with the smooth side used to pound meat and poultry to an even thickness, and the spiked side used for tenderizing tough cuts of meat. This tool is commonly available in either stainless steel or wood.

MEAT THERMOMETER

Meat thermometers take the guesswork out of cooking meats such as roasts and turkeys. A meat thermometer gives an accurate reading of the internal temperature of meat, telling you if it is finished cooking. Meat thermometers are available in manual and digital versions, and some ovens even have built-in meat thermometers.

POTATO MASHER

When making mashed potatoes or egg salad sandwiches, a potato masher will come in handy. Potato mashers are commonly stainless steel, with a plastic handle.

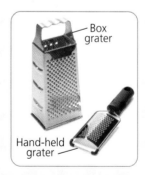

GRATERS

You will need two different sized graters stocked in your kitchen. First, a box grater with medium sized holes will coarsely grate foods such as cheese. Secondly, you will need a hand-held grater with small holes to grate foods like ginger.

CITRUS ZESTER

When a recipe calls for citrus zest, this handy tool will make the job easy. A citrus zester easily removes thin strips of peel from citrus fruit. You can find citrus zesters in many variations, with even the most inexpensive versions working well.

REAMER

For those who love freshly squeezed juice, a reamer is a necessity. Available in wood, ceramic and metal versions, reamers are used to squeeze the juice from citrus fruits.

TONGS

Tongs are useful for handling cooked foods such as pasta, meats and vegetables without piercing the foods. Stainless steel tongs are preferred due to their ease of use.

WOODEN SPOONS

Wooden spoons are a necessity for stirring foods since they are useable in all materials, from aluminum to non-stick cookware. You can find wooden spoons in a variety of shapes and sizes.

SERVING SPOONS

After preparing a delicious meal, you will need serving spoons to dish out the food. You should have both solid and slotted serving spoons. Slotted spoons are useful for removing foods from a pot while leaving the liquid behind.

LARGE PERFORATED SKIMMER

This tool comes in handy for transferring foods from boiling water. When purchasing a perforated skimmer, make sure that it is not too large to fit into your pots. A skimmer between 6 and 8 inches in diameter should work well.

LADLE

Used to dish out foods such as soups, ladles are available in a variety of sizes. You should have at least one 4-ounce ladle for serving soup.

LIFTING SPATULA

When cooking eggs, pancakes or hamburgers, you'll need a lifting spatula to turn the food over during cooking. Lifting spatulas are flat and usually have squared-off edges.

PARCHMENT PAPER

Parchment paper is a grease-resistant paper utilized in cooking and baking. It is often used to line baking sheets and cake pans to keep foods and baked goods from sticking.

MELON BALLER

A tool used to scoop round or oval pieces out of melons. This tool can also be used to scoop the cores out of pears and apples.

Knives

In the kitchen, the knife, in its various forms, is a very important tool.

Most knife blades today are made of either high-carbon stainless steel or carbon steel. High-carbon stainless steel is ideal because it is rust resistant and won't react with foods. Carbon steel, on the other hand, can rust and react with acidic foods leaving them with a metallic taste. Carbon steel also turns some cut vegetables brown.

It's best to buy knives made by companies that specialize in knife manufacturing and remember that it's quality not quantity that counts. You need just three knives to get started—a chef's knife, a bread knife and a paring knife—so buy the best you can afford. Think twice about buying a large set of knives that probably contains several knives you won't use. As your experience grows, you can buy additional knives.

Buying a Knife

- When shopping, pick up a knife you are thinking of buying to ensure you can comfortably grip the handle. The knife should also feel well balanced—that is, the weight of the knife should be evenly distributed between the handle and the blade.

- The knife you choose should have a high-carbon stainless steel blade. High-carbon stainless steel is rust resistant and does not react adversely with food.

- Buy good quality knives. They will be more enjoyable to use and will last for many years.

Chef's Knife

- A chef's knife is the most important knife in the kitchen. This knife can be used for a wide variety of cutting jobs, including mincing garlic, chopping vegetables and carving meat.

- A chef's knife is a large, weighty knife with a blade that is usually 8 to 10 inches long.

- Your knife collection should include a good quality chef's knife.

Where should I store my knives?

To keep your fingers safe and your knives in good condition, you should store your knives in a wooden knife block that sits on your countertop or in a knife tray that fits into a kitchen drawer. A knife tray is a wooden tray with individual slots for storing knives.

You should not store your knives loose in a utensil drawer as your blades may become damaged from hitting other utensils and you may inadvertently cut yourself when searching for utensils.

How should I care for my knives?

When you finish using a knife, it is best to immediately wash it under warm running water, using a soft cloth or paper towel and mild soap. Then dry the knife and put it away. Hand washing will extend the life of your knives.

Do not put your knives in the dishwasher or in a sink filled with water and other dishes. Your knife blades may become damaged from hitting other utensils, pots or dishes and you may inadvertently cut yourself when reaching into the dishwasher or sink.

Bread Knife

Paring Knife

- A bread knife has a serrated, or notched, blade that can slice through food such as bread, loaf cakes and tomatoes without crushing or tearing the food.

- A bread knife has a blade that is usually 8 to 10 inches long.
- Your knife collection should include a bread knife.

- A paring knife is a small knife with a blade that is usually 2 to 4 inches long. This knife can be used for many tasks, including peeling and coring fruit and slicing mushrooms.

- Your knife collection should include at least one paring knife.

Cookware

You can't get cooking without cookware. When selecting cookware such as saucepans, sauté pans and roasting pans, hold the pans in your hand to make sure they feel heavy and sturdy. Also consider the metal of the cookware. Avoid cookware made from uncoated aluminum— it will react with acidic ingredients, like vinegars and tomatoes, and will cause food to turn gray and have a metallic taste.

If you are looking to purchase stainless steel pots, buy those that have an aluminum or copper core throughout the bottom and, preferably, the sides of the pot for even heat distribution. When purchasing cookware, also look for ovenproof handles that will allow you to easily move your pots and pans from the stovetop into the oven.

Stockpots & Dutch Ovens

Stockpot

Dutch oven

Saucepans

4-quart saucepan

2-quart saucepan

Stockpots

- A stockpot is a large pot with a tight-fitting lid that can be used to cook soups, stews and pasta.

- You should have a stockpot with a capacity of at least 8 quarts.

Dutch Ovens

- Dutch ovens are often used for the same purposes as stockpots, but their wider and shallower shape makes them more suitable for oven use.

- You should have a Dutch oven with a capacity of at least 6 quarts.

Saucepans

- Saucepans have long handles and tight-fitting lids.

- You should have one 4-quart saucepan for boiling potatoes and simmering rice.

- You should also have at least one 2-quart saucepan for making sauces and heating soups.

Is there anything else I need in my cookware collection?

Your cookware collection should include a steamer that you can use to steam food such as vegetables and dumplings. There are several types of steamers available. Some saucepans include a steamer insert that looks like a pot and has a lid and handles. A collapsible stainless steel steamer basket expands to fit into saucepans of different sizes, while a steamer made from bamboo sits on top of a saucepan.

Steamer insert

Bamboo steamer

Collapsible steamer basket

Sauté Pans

Skillets

Nonstick skillet

Uncoated skillet

Roasting Pans & Roasting Racks

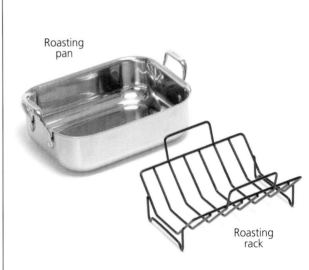

Roasting pan

Roasting rack

Sauté Pans

- A sauté pan with a tight-fitting lid is very versatile and can be used for simmering chicken dishes or poaching fish.

- Your sauté pan should have a capacity of 5 to 6 quarts and should have an uncoated surface.

Skillets

- Skillets, also called frying pans, can have a nonstick or uncoated surface.

- You should have one nonstick or uncoated 6-inch skillet and at least one uncoated skillet measuring 10 to 12 inches in diameter.

Roasting Pans

- Roasting pans are pans used for roasting meat and poultry as well as baking lasagna.

- You should have one medium-sized roasting pan that measures approximately 15x10 inches.

Roasting Racks

- A roasting rack is a metal rack that is placed in the bottom of a roasting pan to keep food off the bottom of the pan. A roasting rack allows excess fat and juices to drain away from the food and helps promote even cooking.

Bakeware

Bakeware includes items such as baking sheets, cake pans and loaf pans. Before purchasing bakeware, you should handle the items. The pans and sheets should feel heavy and thick, not flimsy and lightweight. Quality bakeware should last for many years, and flimsy or lightweight items can buckle from oven heat and dent easily. To avoid burning your baked goods, you should stay away from black-colored pans, which tend to attract more heat and may burn the bottoms of cookies and cakes. Also remember that the surfaces of nonstick pans tend to scratch easily. To prevent scratches, you can use parchment paper on non-stick surfaces. Lastly, try thinking outside of the pan: in addition to being used to bake desserts, some bakeware can also be used to cook other types of food in the oven, like fish, chicken and pasta.

Bakeware is available in a variety of different materials.

Baking Sheets

Cooling Racks

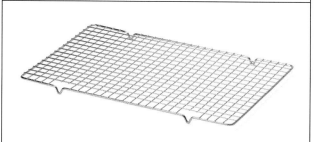

Round Cake Pans

Square & Rectangular Baking Pans

Square baking pan

Rectangular baking pan

Baking Sheets

- Also known as cookie sheets, these rectangular metal pans can be used to bake cookies as well as broil fish. You should have at least two baking sheets.

- Make sure the baking sheets you choose will fit into your oven. Also, choose baking sheets with 1/2-inch high sides.

Cooling Racks

- Once removed from their pan, baked goods can be placed onto cooling racks. This allows air to circulate around baked goods as they cool.

- You should have one large cooling rack.

Round Cake Pans

- Round cake pans can be used to make layer cakes.

- You should have two round cake pans measuring 8 or 9 inches in diameter.

Square & Rectangular Baking Pans

- Square and rectangular baking pans can be used to bake desserts. These pans can also be used to bake chicken and pasta dishes.

- You should have at least one 8x8 or 9x9 inch square pan and at least one 9x13 inch rectangular pan.

Tip

Are there any other items I should have in my bakeware collection?

Yes. A 9-inch springform pan and a tube pan. A springform pan is round, with removable sides for easy removal of delicate cakes. You should choose a springform pan that is 9-inches wide. A tube pan, also known as an angel food or sponge cake pan, is a deep, round pan with a hollow tube in the center. Some tube pans have removable bottoms so you can easily remove the cake.

Tube pan

Springform pan

Muffin Pans

Loaf Pans

Pie Plates

Covered Casserole Dishes

Muffin Pans

- A muffin pan, also called a muffin tin, has individual cups used for baking muffins and cupcakes.

- You should have at least one muffin pan that makes 12 large muffins.

Loaf Pans

- Loaf pans can be used to bake bread, pound cakes and meatloaf.

- Your bakeware collection should include at least two 8x4x2½ or 9x5x3 inch loaf pans.

Pie Plates

- Pie plates, also called pie pans, are used to bake pies. Tempered glass pie plates are recommended because they offer even heat distribution.

- Your bakeware collection should include a pie plate measuring 8 or 9 inches in diameter.

Covered Casserole Dishes

- Covered casserole dishes can be used to make puddings and noodle casseroles.

- You should have a 3-quart and a 5-quart covered casserole dish.

Appliances

Every kitchen needs a refrigerator, stove and microwave. Beyond these essentials, however, there are several other appliances you should have on hand to help with food preparation.

A well-equipped kitchen should have a food processor to chop, grate, mix and shred ingredients at the touch of a button.

You should also have at least one blender—either a small immersion blender or a countertop blender. Many people find immersion blenders handy because they can blend ingredients right in the pot.

It is also important to have at least one type of mixer—a hand mixer or a stand mixer. A hand mixer is smaller and easier to store, while a larger stand mixer is advantageous because it can work unattended while you perform other tasks.

Well-Equipped Kitchen

- In addition to your refrigerator, stove and microwave, there are several other appliances you should have in your kitchen.

- A well-equipped kitchen should have a food processor along with at least one type of blender and mixer.

- The amount of counter space you have and how you plan to use the appliance will help determine which blender and mixer are right for you.

Food Processors

- A food processor is an efficient and versatile appliance that can make quick work of many tasks including making pie dough, chopping nuts, slicing vegetables and grating cheese or carrots. Food processors can also blend and purée ingredients.

- Using a food processor can significantly reduce the amount of time and energy you spend on food preparation. A food processor with a 10 to 12 cup capacity is appropriate for most home applications.

Are there any other appliances I should have?

Consider also purchasing a toaster oven. A toaster oven is a miniature oven that sits on your countertop. It is useful for small jobs when you do not want to turn on your full-size oven. For example, baked potatoes, pizza and toasted open-faced sandwiches can be cooked in a toaster oven.

Blenders

Immersion Blender

Blender

Mixers

Hand Mixer

Stand Mixer

Immersion Blender
- An immersion blender is a small, hand-held blender that is placed directly into a large bowl or saucepan to blend or purée the contents.
- Immersion blenders are handy for light jobs such as puréeing soups.

Blender
- A blender is more powerful than an immersion blender and sits on your countertop.
- Blenders can perform heavy-duty tasks such as chopping ice, blending fruit smoothies as well as puréeing and liquefying ingredients.

Hand Mixer
- A hand mixer, also called a beater, is a small appliance used to perform light tasks such as beating egg whites, whipping cream and mixing cake batters.

Stand Mixer
- A stand mixer is a large, powerful mixer that sits on your countertop. Stand mixers perform light mixing duties as well as heavy mixing duties.
- A stand mixer is recommended for anyone who plans to bake extensively.

Organizing Your Kitchen

You may not be able to change the location of your refrigerator or sink, but there is a kitchen renovation that can make your space much more efficient—and it's free! By simply changing where your kitchen tools, foods and small appliances reside, you can make your kitchen feel brand new.

The key to making your kitchen more efficient is to move your pots, pans and utensils to locations where they will be used most often.

This will save you leg work and take a lot of effort out of cooking. Keeping often-used small appliances on the counter will also save time and energy.

As a general rule, just remember to keep items used for similar tasks together. For example, keep your pots and pans together and store them near the stove.

Do not store food by the stove that will be negatively affected by the heat from the stove.

Countertop

Small Appliances

- Use an area of countertop close to your stove for food preparation.

- Keep your countertop free of clutter such as mail or magazines. This saves you from having to tidy up before you begin cooking.

- Keep an area of countertop close to your stove free of appliances and other objects so you can place utensils and hot pots and pans there as you cook.

  Note: Use hot pads under hot pots and pans to protect your countertop.

- Store small appliances you use regularly on your countertop. This will make them more accessible.

- Remove appliances you rarely use from your countertop and store them in a cabinet.

- If possible, place your toaster, coffee maker and kettle together on your countertop. This creates an efficient breakfast station.

- If possible, place your stand mixer and food processor close to the cabinet that stores your baking ingredients. This creates an efficient baking station.

What should I store in the cabinet under my sink?

You should not use the cabinet under your sink for anything other than storing cleaning supplies and garbage. This area is prone to high humidity and occasional leaks.

Never store cleaning supplies together with any type of food. Cleaning supplies and detergents can be extremely toxic. If you have young children or pets and use the cabinet under the sink to store cleaning supplies, this cabinet should have a child-safety lock.

What should I have on hand around my sink?

You should always have liquid hand-washing soap at the sink ready for use. This will help to establish a habit of washing your hands in hot, soapy water before, during and after cooking. Liquid dish detergent and paper towels should also be kept near the sink. This will make cleaning up more efficient. Also consider having a drying rack in your sink. Air drying dishes and utensils requires no effort on your part and is a hygienic way to dry your dishes.

Cookware, Utensils and Dishes

Spices and Pantry Items

- Store utensils, such as tongs and wooden spoons, close to the stove in a container on your countertop or hung on the wall.
- Store pots and pans, along with their lids, close to the stove.

- Store knives close to your food preparation area in a wooden knife block on your countertop or in a knife tray inside a drawer.
- Store dishes and glasses in a cabinet close to the dishwasher.

- Store salt and pepper on your countertop close to the stove.
- Store spices and dried herbs close to the stove in a spice rack or cabinet.

- Store often used condiments such as oils, vinegars and soy sauce, in a cabinet close to the food preparation area and stove.
- Group and store related foods together. For example, store all your canned goods together and store all of your baking ingredients together.

Reading a Recipe

Most of us are not comfortable enough to whip up a dinner off the top of our heads. That's why we have recipes. A recipe is merely a set of instructions for preparing food. Once you know how to read a recipe, you can cook just about anything.

Your first step with any recipe should be to read it from start to finish. By reading ahead, you can make sure that you understand all the steps, have all the ingredients and have enough time to prepare the recipe.

INGREDIENT LIST

The ingredient list tells you which ingredients you'll need and how much of each one is required.

You may notice that some ingredients are listed as "optional." These ingredients are not essential, but can give the dish more flavor, texture or visual appeal.

When the list gives a choice of ingredients, such as "shredded cheddar or mozzarella cheese," the first item is the preferred ingredient.

Some ingredients also include directions. Pay special attention to how ingredients with directions are worded. For example, "1 cup chopped walnuts" is a cup of walnuts that have been chopped before measuring, but "1 cup walnuts, chopped" is a cup of walnuts measured whole and then chopped.

GETTING STARTED

Before you start cooking, you should set out on your counter all of the ingredients, utensils, cookware and bakeware called for in the recipe. This will save you from trying to find an ingredient or utensil in a panic while something on the stove is starting to burn.

The ingredients should be measured out exactly as listed, prepared as specified (for example, one egg, beaten) and at the temperature outlined. Most recipes list ingredients in the order in which they are used, and you should organize them on your counter in the same manner. Once everything is in its place and ready to go, you can start cooking!

Asian Chicken Stir-Fry

This Asian Chicken Stir-Fry combines crisp vegetables, tender chicken strips and fabulous Asian flavors. Instead of purchasing chicken strips, which can be expensive, simply buy 1 pound of boneless chicken breasts and cut them into 1/4-inch strips. The secret to a great stir-fry is to have all of the ingredients ready before you start cooking. There won't be any time for cutting vegetables once your sauté pan is hot.

Makes 4 servings

INGREDIENTS
1/4 cup oyster sauce
2 tablespoons soy sauce
2 garlic cloves, minced
3 tablespoons extra virgin olive oil
1 pound chicken stir-fry strips
1 medium onion, cut into 1/2-inch slices
1/2 pound fresh snow peas, strings removed
1 medium zucchini, cut into sticks
1 red pepper, cut into strips
1 can (14 ounces) baby corn, drained and rinsed (optional)

Asian Chicken Stir-Fry

1 In a small bowl, combine the oyster sauce, soy sauce and garlic using a whisk. Set aside.

2 Heat a large sauté pan over medium-high heat for 1 to 2 minutes.

3 Add 2 tablespoons of the oil to the pan and heat up for 20 seconds.

4 Add the chicken strips to the pan and cook, tossing continuously with two wooden spoons, until no longer pink, about 3 to 4 minutes. Place into a bowl and set aside.

5 Add the remaining 1 tablespoon of oil to the pan.

6 Add the onion and snow peas to the pan and cook, tossing continuously for 2 minutes.

188

SERVINGS

Most recipes will indicate the approximate number of servings the recipe will make.

28

NUTRITIONAL INFORMATION

Recipes often list nutritional information for the dish. This provides you with information such as the amount of calories, fat, carbohydrates, dietary fiber and protein in each serving. This information can be especially important for people who are following special diets, such as reduced-fat or low-sodium diets.

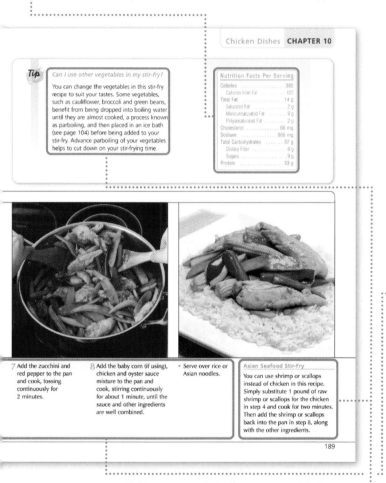

Tip

Can I use other vegetables in my stir-fry?

You can change the vegetables in this stir-fry recipe to suit your tastes. Some vegetables, such as cauliflower, broccoli and green beans, benefit from being dropped into boiling water until they are almost cooked, a process known as parboiling, and then placed in an ice bath (see page 104) before being added to your stir-fry. Advance parboiling of your vegetables helps to cut down on your stir-frying time.

Nutrition Facts Per Serving

Calories	385
Calories from Fat	122
Total Fat	14 g
Saturated Fat	2 g
Monounsaturated Fat	9 g
Polyunsaturated Fat	2 g
Cholesterol	66 mg
Sodium	866 mg
Total Carbohydrates	37 g
Dietary Fiber	6 g
Sugars	9 g
Protein	33 g

7 Add the zucchini and red pepper to the pan and cook, tossing continuously for 2 minutes.

8 Add the baby corn (if using), chicken and oyster sauce mixture to the pan and cook, stirring continuously for about 1 minute, until the sauce and other ingredients are well combined.

• Serve over rice or Asian noodles.

Asian Seafood Stir-Fry

You can use shrimp or scallops instead of chicken in this recipe. Simply substitute 1 pound of raw shrimp or scallops for the chicken in step 4 and cook for two minutes. Then add the shrimp or scallops back into the pan in step 8, along with the other ingredients.

189

SERVING SUGGESTIONS AND RECIPE VARIATIONS

Many recipes suggest ways of serving a dish or foods that can be served alongside it. Recipes can also suggest different ingredients or an alternate method of preparing the recipe. These variations allow you to create a number of different-tasting dishes from just one recipe.

STANDARD INGREDIENTS (IN THIS BOOK)

Some ingredients come in different forms, which can make a significant difference in how a dish turns out. To make sure that readers are all using the same ingredients, cookbooks outline their own set of standard ingredients. Unless otherwise specified, when recipes in this book call for:

- Milk – use 1% milk.
- Pepper – use freshly ground black pepper.
- Eggs – use large eggs.
- Butter – use unsalted butter.
- Salt – use table salt.
- Chicken, beef or vegetable broth – use store-bought broth.
- Lemon or lime juice – use freshly-squeezed juice.

DIRECTIONS

It's important to follow all the directions for a recipe carefully and in the order they appear.

All cooking should be done in uncovered pots and pans, unless specified otherwise.

Be sure to follow all suggested oven and stovetop temperatures. When using the oven, make sure the oven has reached the correct temperature before putting the food in and always use the center oven rack, unless specified otherwise.

Weather, altitude and even the equipment being used can affect cooking times. To account for this, many recipes suggest a range of cooking times and may also include important cues that indicate the way food should look or feel, such as "sauté until lightly browned." You should start checking the look or feel at the earliest time indicated in the recipe to determine doneness.

Measuring Ingredients

Ingredients are normally measured with cups and spoons of specific sizes. Dry-ingredient measuring cups are used to measure both dry ingredients, like flour, and semi-solid ingredients, like shortening. Liquid-ingredient measuring cups are used to measure liquids, like milk. Small amounts of dry, semi-solid and liquid ingredients, such as spices, butter and oil, are measured with measuring spoons.

There are a few guidelines for measuring that you should keep in mind. Avoid measuring ingredients over a mixing bowl in case the measuring cup or spoon overflows—measure ingredients over their container or waxed paper instead. Always spoon or scoop dry ingredients into a measuring cup to avoid overpacking. Don't shake or tap measuring cups or spoons—this leads to inaccurate measurements.

Flour should be stirred before measuring to ensure it is not packed down.

Measuring Dry Ingredients

Step 1

Step 2

Measuring Semi-Solid Ingredients

Step 1

Step 3

- Dry measuring cups are commonly available in sets of 1/4 cup, 1/3 cup, 1/2 cup and 1 cup sizes and are used to measure ingredients such as flour or sugar.

1 Use a scoop or spoon to place the ingredient into a dry measuring cup until the ingredient is slightly above the rim of the cup. Do not shake or tap the measuring cup.

2 Move the straight edge of a table knife across the rim of the measuring cup to level off the dry ingredient.

- You can also use dry measuring cups to measure semi-solid ingredients such as peanut butter or shortening.

1 Use a rubber spatula to place the ingredient into a dry measuring cup, pressing the ingredient down into the cup to remove any air pockets.

2 Repeat step 1 until the semi-solid ingredient is slightly above the rim of the measuring cup.

3 Move the straight edge of a table knife across the rim of the measuring cup to level off the semi-solid ingredient.

How do I measure brown sugar?

Brown sugar should always be firmly pressed into a measuring cup and then leveled off with a table knife. Since brown sugar is best stored in a resealable plastic bag to prevent it from hardening, you can measure directly inside the bag. Put the measuring cup or spoon into the bag and, with your hand on the outside of the bag, firmly pack the sugar into the cup or spoon. Then use the straight edge of a table knife to level off the sugar inside the bag.

How do I measure 1/8 teaspoon or a pinch?

If a recipe calls for 1/8 teaspoon and you do not have the right size measuring spoon, fill a 1/4-teaspoon measuring spoon only half full. A pinch is exactly what it sounds like—the amount of a dry ingredient that you can pinch between your index finger and thumb. A pinch measures out to about 1/16 teaspoon.

Measuring Liquid Ingredients

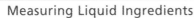

Using Measuring Spoons

- Liquid measuring cups are commonly available in 1 cup, 2 cup and 4 cup sizes and are used to measure ingredients such as milk or water.

1 Place a liquid measuring cup on your countertop.

2 Pour the liquid into the measuring cup until the liquid reaches the desired measurement.

3 To ensure the accuracy of the measurement, bend down as you pour so you can read the measurement at eye level.

- Measuring spoons are commonly available in the following sets: 1/4 teaspoon (tsp), 1/2 teaspoon, 1 teaspoon and 1 tablespoon (tbsp).

1 To measure a dry or semi-solid ingredient, use the measuring spoon to scoop out the ingredient. Then move the straight edge of a table knife across the rim of the spoon to level off the ingredient.

- To measure a liquid ingredient, pour the ingredient into the measuring spoon.

Knife Skills

A sharp knife is an indispensable tool in the kitchen. With proper knife-handling techniques, you can avoid injury and learn to prepare food with ease.

When cutting, the motion of each cut should be away from your body. After making a cut, move your hand holding the food back along the food to make just enough space for the next cut.

When walking with a knife, hold it steady at your side, pointing downward, with the sharp edge facing behind you. If you have to pass a knife to another person, set it down on the counter with the handle facing the other person.

Dull knives can unexpectedly slip off of food and injure you. It is advisable to purchase a tool called a sharpening steel, which helps to keep the edge of your knives sharp. You should hone your knives with a sharpening steel regularly, well before they begin to feel dull. With regular honing, your knives should need professional sharpening only once or twice a year.

Handling a Knife

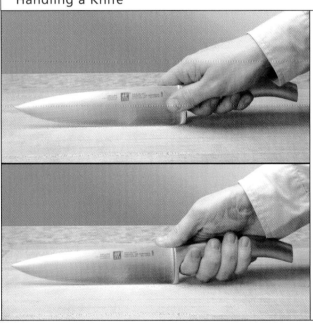

Thumb behind index finger

First knuckle

- A common way to hold a knife is to grasp the heel of the blade between your thumb and index finger with the remaining 3 fingers wrapped around the handle.

- This grip will give you the most control for most situations.

- Another way to hold a knife is to place your thumb along the top of the blade, while wrapping your other 4 fingers around the handle.

- This grip is useful for cuts that require more force, such as cutting through squash.

- When holding food you want to cut, your fingers should be curled slightly back with the tips pointing back toward the palm of your hand. Your thumb should be positioned behind your index finger.

- The first knuckle of your fingers should be placed against the broad side of the knife's blade while you are cutting.

- As you make each cut, do not raise the sharp edge of the knife higher than the level of the first knuckle of your fingers.

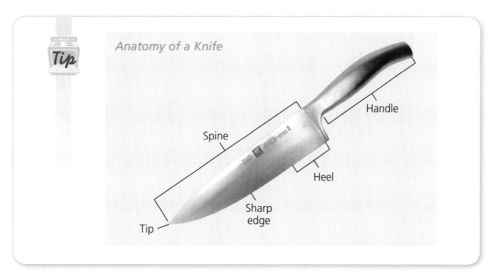

Anatomy of a Knife

Handle

Spine

Heel

Tip

Sharp edge

Hone a Knife

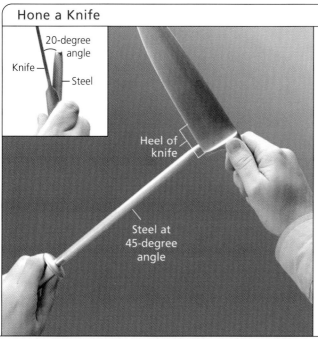

20-degree angle

Knife

Steel

Heel of knife

Steel at 45-degree angle

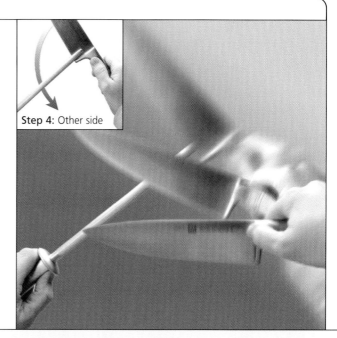

Step 4: Other side

- These instructions are for a right-handed individual.

- This technique cannot be used to hone serrated knives.

1 Hold the sharpening steel in front of you with your left hand. Point the tip of the steel up to the right at a 45-degree angle.

2 Using your right hand, place the heel of the knife at the tip of the steel. The sharp edge should be resting against the steel at a 20-degree angle.

3 Pivot the wrist of your right hand downward, carefully running the entire sharp edge of the knife along the length of the steel toward the steel's handle. It is important to maintain the 20-degree angle between the knife and the steel.

- Only the knife should move while honing. The steel and your left arm should remain stationary.

4 Repeat step 3 another 5 or 6 times, alternating from one side of the knife to the other.

5 Wash and dry the knife to remove any metal particles.

Handling Food Safely

Harmful bacteria can lurk on food, your utensils and even your hands. You cannot normally see, taste or smell it, but harmful bacteria can make you quite ill if eaten. Fortunately, there are four simple guidelines to keep your food safe.

Clean: Wash hands, surfaces and equipment often and immediately after they come in contact with raw meat, poultry, seafood or eggs. For example, if you use tongs to handle raw meat, you must clean the tongs before using them to handle cooked meat.

Separate: Keep raw meats, poultry, fish and eggs separate from other raw or cooked foods to prevent cross contamination, the spreading of harmful bacteria from one food to another food or piece of equipment.

Cook: Cooking foods to the proper temperature kills harmful bacteria. A meat thermometer is essential to ensure that food has been properly cooked.

Chill: Always refrigerate perishable foods and leftovers promptly to keep harmful bacteria from multiplying.

Clean

- Wash your hands using hot, soapy water before preparing food and immediately after handling raw meat, poultry, seafood or eggs.
- Before food preparation, use fabric dishcloths to wash your countertop, clean your cutting board, knives and utensils. Avoid using sponges.
- Immediately after coming into contact with raw meat, poultry, seafood and eggs, you should use disposable paper towels to wash your countertop, cutting board, knives and utensils.

Separate

- The spread of bacteria from raw meat, poultry, seafood or eggs to other food and equipment in your kitchen is called cross contamination. There are a couple of things you can do to prevent cross contamination.
- Use a separate cutting board for cutting only raw meat, poultry and seafood.
- Store raw meat, poultry and seafood in containers on the bottom shelf of your fridge so their juices do not drip onto other foods.

Will rinsing meat and poultry before cooking remove bacteria?

You should not rinse raw meat and poultry since washing does not remove bacteria from these foods. Cooking to the appropriate temperature is the only way to effectively eliminate harmful bacteria. By rinsing meat and poultry before cooking, you risk cross contamination by spreading bacteria to your sink and countertop.

How do I safely thaw meat, poultry and seafood?

Thawing food in the refrigerator is the safest method for defrosting. Wrapped meat, poultry and seafood should be set on the bottom shelf of your fridge in a container, such as a bowl or baking pan, so the juices do not drip onto other foods. You should never defrost food on your countertop because bacteria multiplies very quickly at room temperature. Partially thawed meat, poultry and seafood should not be refrozen.

Cook

Chill

- Cooking meat and poultry to the proper temperature will kill any harmful bacteria the food may contain.

- Use a clean meat thermometer to check the internal temperature of meat and poultry to determine when it is cooked. Insert the meat thermometer into the center of the food, away from any bones, and wait approximately 30 seconds.

- Cook cuts of pork and ground meats to 160°F. Cook ground poultry to 165°F, poultry breasts to 170°F and whole poultry to 180°F.

- Do not overstock your refrigerator. Cold air must be able to circulate to keep food cold.

- Do not put hot food directly into your freezer. Refrigerate it first. Hot food could cause the food in your freezer to partially thaw.

- Your refrigerator should be set at 40°F or below. You can use a refrigerator thermometer to check your refrigerator's temperature.

- Refrigerate leftovers within two hours of cooking. Separate large amounts of leftovers into small, shallow containers to help them cool more quickly.

Stocking Your Refrigerator & Freezer

Your refrigerator is designed to keep your food in tip-top condition.

The refrigerator is the best place to store perishable foods, opened condiments and fresh fruits and vegetables. It will preserve their freshness and prevent spoilage. The freezer is where you can store items that you want to have on hand for an extended period of time.

You should sort through the contents of your refrigerator on a regular basis and discard rotten fruits and vegetables, spoiled cheeses and any food that has passed its best before date. You should also sort through the contents of your freezer regularly and throw out any items that have freezer burn—you'll notice a discolored and dry appearance on items that have freezer burn.

To cook a wide variety of dishes, there are several items you should always have on hand in your refrigerator and freezer. The following discusses the basics you will need.

REFRIGERATOR ESSENTIALS

EGGS & DAIRY PRODUCTS

Eggs: Eggs are easy to prepare in a variety of ways and a key ingredient in many baking recipes. Keep raw eggs in their original carton on an inside shelf.

1% Milk: Milk is a basic ingredient called for in many baking and cooking recipes.

Cheese: It's handy to have a selection of cheeses on hand—consider cheddar, mozzarella and parmesan. Cheese is great for use in many recipes, such as omelets and pasta dishes.

Butter or Margarine: Butter or margarine can be used for general cooking purposes. Butter and margarine should be stored in their original packaging or a sealed container in the refrigerator.

FRUITS & VEGETABLES

In addition to the fruits and vegetables you eat on a daily basis, you should have the following on hand.

Carrots and Celery: Often used together, carrots and celery create the flavor base of many recipes, including sauces and soups. Carrots and celery should be stored in the vegetable drawer in plastic bags.

Lemons: Fresh lemon juice and lemon zest are ingredients in many recipes. Lemon juice is also useful for preventing peeled or cut fruits from turning brown.

Salad Greens: Salad greens should be kept in their original packaging or in a plastic vegetable bag and stored in the vegetable drawer.

FREEZER ESSENTIALS

MEAT

You may want to have several packages of the cuts of meat and poultry you use most often in the freezer.

Chicken: Having a few packages of chicken in the freezer is always a good idea. Chicken is very versatile and can be used in many recipes.

Beef: Ground beef is very handy to have in the freezer. It can be defrosted to make dishes like meatloaf and chili.

Pork: Both pork chops and pork tenderloin are small cuts of meat that do not take up much freezer space and can be defrosted and cooked for an easy midweek meal.

FRUITS & VEGETABLES

Frozen fruits and vegetables are practical and convenient. Often when some types of fruits and vegetables are not available fresh, they can be found in the freezer section of the grocery store. For example, berries are not always in season, but they can almost always be found frozen.

Look for frozen fruits and vegetables that are packed in a resealable plastic bag. This allows you to pour out what you need and return the unused portion to the freezer quickly.

Frozen Vegetables: You should have packages of frozen peas, corn, green beans and mixed vegetables on hand in your freezer. They are great for using as side dishes, in stir-fries and added to soups.

Frozen Fruit: It's a good idea to have packages of frozen fruit such as blueberries, cranberries, raspberries and mixed fruit in your freezer. Buy them unsweetened so you can better control the sugar content of your dishes.

BAKING & COOKING NEEDS

Butter: Unsalted butter is preferred for baking. Salt acts as a preservative, so unsalted butter is more perishable than the salted variety. To keep unsalted butter fresh for a period of time, store unused portions in the freezer.

Ice: Make sure your ice cube trays/bin are filled. You will need ice in cooking more often than you can imagine.

Nuts: A selection of pecans, walnuts and almonds is nice to have on hand. These nuts can be used for baking. For long-term storage, place nuts in a resealable plastic bag, squeeze out the air and then place in the freezer.

Bread Crumbs: Bread crumbs can be used to bread meat and poultry. In an airtight container, bread crumbs will last in the freezer for up to six months.

Stocking Your Pantry

Traditionally, a pantry referred to a room or closet set aside for storing dry goods. Today, a pantry is any cool, dry, dark area in your kitchen, such as a cupboard, where you store ingredients that do not require refrigeration.

The following is a list of ingredients that are commonly used in recipes. Keeping these staple ingredients in your pantry will save you from having to run out to the store each time you're ready to cook or bake.

GENERAL COOKING & BAKING ESSENTIALS

The following ingredients are frequently used when cooking and baking. Unopened items can be stored in their original containers. After opening, store these items in clear, airtight containers or resealable plastic bags.

Sugar: Keep both granulated sugar and light brown sugar on hand.

Flour: All-purpose flour is the best type to have in your pantry. It is used extensively in baking and for breading meat and poultry.

Oatmeal: Quick oats can be used in baked cookies or as an ingredient in meatloaf.

Cornstarch: This ingredient can be used for thickening gravies and sauces and for making shortbread.

Cornmeal: This ingredient can be used to make cornbread or for breading meat.

BAKING NEEDS   These ingredients are a must if you plan to bake.

Baking powder and baking soda: These ingredients act as leavening agents, helping baked goods rise.

Powdered sugar: Used to make frostings. Also called confectioners' sugar or icing sugar.

Vegetable shortening: Used extensively for making flaky pie crusts. Also used for greasing pans. To avoid trans fats, use non-hydrogenated vegetable shortening.

Chocolate products: Unsweetened cocoa, semi-sweet chocolate chips and unsweetened chocolate squares are essential for making cookies and chocolate sauces.

Dried fruit: Keep raisins and other dried fruit, such as apricots and cranberries, on hand.

Pure vanilla extract: A flavoring agent used in desserts and baked goods.

DRIED PASTA, RICE, BEANS & LENTILS

Pasta

There are many different types of pasta available. You should always have at least one variety of long pasta, such as spaghetti, and one variety of short pasta, such as macaroni, in your pantry.

Pasta made from nutritious whole wheat and other whole grains is now readily available. Dried pasta will keep for a long time if stored in an airtight container or sealed plastic bag.

Rice

You should stock your pantry with your choice of long-grain or short-grain rice. Rice is available in both white and brown forms. White rice, once opened, can be stored for 2 years in an airtight container in your pantry. Brown rice, once opened, can be stored for only 6 months in an airtight container in your pantry before spoiling.

Beans

Beans can be served as a side dish or added to other dishes, such as soups and stews. Popular examples of dried beans include kidney beans, pinto beans and navy beans.

Dried beans can be stored in an airtight container for six months to a year. Before cooking, dried beans must be soaked in water for at least eight hours to soften them.

Lentils

Lentils, like beans, are very nutritious and can be served as a side dish or used as an ingredient in salads and soups. There are many varieties of lentils, including green, red and brown.

Lentils can be stored in an airtight container for about a year.

CANNED GOODS

In general, unopened canned goods can be stored for one to two years in your pantry.

Tomatoes and Tomato-Based Products

Keep cans of whole tomatoes, diced tomatoes, tomato sauce, pasta sauce and tomato paste on hand at all times. Whole and diced tomatoes are used in sauces, stews and soups. Tomato sauce and pasta sauce can be used in recipes with pasta. Tomato paste is often used as a flavor base in sauces and stews.

Beans

Keep several cans of beans, such as chickpeas and kidney beans, on hand. Canned beans can be served as a side dish or added to soups and salads.

Broth

Cans or cartons of low-sodium broth are essential for making soups and stews. Once opened, you can store broth in a sealed container in the fridge for about a week or in the freezer for several months. Broth is also available in dried powder and cube form.

Fish

Keep several varieties of canned fish, including salmon, tuna and sardines, in your pantry. Canned fish can be used for making sandwiches and as an ingredient in salads and casseroles.

Fruit

Having a few cans of fruit on hand is a good idea. Canned pineapple, for example, can be used in fruit salads or as a garnish for vegetable and meat dishes. Canned mandarin oranges make a simple, yet delicious, addition to salads.

CONDIMENTS

Condiments are sauces and spreads that are added to other foods to enhance their flavors. Unopened condiments can be stored for about a year in your pantry.

BASIC CONDIMENTS

You should always have basic condiments on hand.

Ketchup, sweet relish and prepared mustard: Used for garnishing hamburgers and hot dogs or in recipes.

Mayonnaise: Used in sandwiches and salads or as a base for dressings.

Dijon mustard: Used as a sandwich spread and in vinaigrettes and sauces.

Liquid honey, maple syrup and jam: Used as a topping or in sauces.

SALSA AND SAUCES

Although some condiments have their roots in ethnic cuisine, they have found their way into many recipes and are handy to have around.

Salsa: A chunky sauce made of tomatoes, onions and peppers that accompanies many Mexican dishes.

Soy sauce or tamari sauce: Used in stir-fries and marinades.

Worcestershire sauce: Used as a flavoring agent in many dishes.

VEGETABLES

Not all vegetables come fresh from the farm. The following vegetables are commonly found packed in jars.

Olives: Used as garnishes and in sauces and salads. There are many different olive varieties available, including green, black and stuffed.

Pickles: Used as a garnish for sandwiches and hamburgers or as an ingredient in potato salad.

OILS

Oil is used daily in most kitchens either as an ingredient or for frying.

Keep several oils, such as safflower or canola oil and all-purpose extra virgin olive oil on hand. You should also keep a bottle of olive oil that is not extra virgin for baking.

GARLIC & ONIONS

Fresh garlic and onions are indispensable in a large number of recipes.

Whole bulbs of garlic and uncut onions can be stored for up to a month in your pantry.

Once onions are cut, they should be stored in the refrigerator for up to 3 days.

VINEGARS

You should have a selection of vinegars on hand. Distilled white vinegar is used to poach eggs and fish. White wine, red wine, sherry, balsamic and cider vinegars can be used for making salad dressings and sauces. Rice vinegar is used for Asian salads and dipping sauces.

DRIED HERBS

A herb is a plant with fragrant leaves that is used to flavor food.

You should keep the following dried herbs in your pantry. After opening, store dried herbs in airtight containers for up to one year, since herbs lose their flavor over time.

For some herbs, such as basil, chives, dill, cilantro and parsley, purchase the herbs fresh rather than dried since they taste much better fresh.

HERB	FORM	DESCRIPTION
Bay Leaves	Whole leaves	Potent flavor. Commonly used in stews. Remove from dish before serving.
Italian Seasoning	Leaves	A blend of herbs, including oregano and rosemary. Commonly used in sauces.
Marjoram	Leaves	Sweet, woodsy flavor. Commonly used in fish dishes, tomato sauces and stews.
Oregano	Leaves	Earthy flavor. Commonly used in tomato sauces and meat dishes.
Rosemary	Leaves	Pine flavor. Commonly used in vegetable and grilled meat dishes.
Sage	Ground	Slightly bitter. Commonly used in stuffings, as well as poultry and fish dishes.
Thyme	Leaves	Lemon and mint flavor. Commonly used in fish, meat and poultry dishes.

SPICES

Spices are used to enhance the taste of food. Spices come in various forms, from whole to ground. You should keep the following spices in your pantry and replace them one year after opening.

HERB	FORM & DESCRIPTION	HERB	FORM & DESCRIPTION
Allspice	Ground A flavor resembling a combination of cinnamon, nutmeg and cloves. Commonly used in baked goods.	Garlic Powder	Ground Concentrated garlic flavor. Commonly used in salad dressings and marinades.
Ancho Chili Powder	Ground Mildly hot and sweet flavor. Commonly used in chili, marinades, soups and stews.	Ginger	Ground Warm, tangy flavor. Commonly used in baked goods as well as fish, meat and vegetable dishes.
Cayenne Pepper	Ground Hot, spicy flavor. Made from chili peppers. Commonly used in salsa and marinades.	Nutmeg	Whole or ground Sweet, spicy flavor. Commonly used in baked goods, sauces and soups. Best when freshly grated.
Cinnamon	Sticks and ground Sweet, woodsy flavor. Commonly used in baked goods.	Onion Powder	Ground Concentrated sweet onion flavor. Commonly used in salad dressings and marinades.
Cloves	Whole and ground Strong, sweet flavor. Commonly used in pork, beef and vegetable dishes.	Paprika	Ground Ranges from sweet to hot. Commonly used in dips and soups.
Coriander Seed	Ground Warm, earthy flavor. Commonly used in curries, Mexican foods and pork dishes.	Pepper	Peppercorns or ground Available in many varieties, but black pepper is most commonly used. Best when freshly ground.
Cumin	Ground Warm, nutty flavor. Commonly used in curry, fish, poultry and beef dishes.	Red Pepper	Flakes Hot, spicy flavor. Commonly used in salsa, chili and chicken and beef dishes.
Curry Powder	Ground Ranges from mild to spicy. Commonly used in curry, chicken and rice dishes.	Salt	Crystals Includes table, kosher, sea and seasoned salt. Seasoned salt is a blend of ingredients including salt, paprika, garlic powder and onion powder.
Dry Mustard	Ground Spicy, sharp flavor. Commonly used in meat and vegetable dishes as well as marinades.	Turmeric	Ground Aromatic, earthy flavor. Commonly used in curry, rice and poultry dishes.

Types of Rice

For nearly half of the world's population, rice is a part of daily life. In fact, thousands of different varieties of rice are grown around the world.

Rice contains no cholesterol, is low in sodium and contains only a tiny bit of fat. The nutritional value of rice varies depending on the type of rice.

TYPES OF RICE

RICE TYPE	DESCRIPTION	TASTE	COOKED TEXTURE	APPEARANCE	SHELF LIFE
White Rice	Also called polished rice, white rice has had the outer husk, bran and germ portions of the grain removed. Because removing the bran and germ also removes much of the nutritional value, white rice is often enriched with nutrients like riboflavin, iron, niacin and thiamin.	Ranges from fragrant to flavorless	Soft but not mushy	White in color	Between one and two years in an airtight container
Brown Rice	Grains of brown rice have had only the inedible outer husk removed, leaving the darker bran and germ portions of the grain intact. As a result, brown rice has more fiber, flavor and nutrients than white rice.	Somewhat nutty	Slightly chewy, not completely soft	Light tan in color	Six months in an airtight container, slightly longer if refrigerated
Converted Rice	Converted rice is a more nutritious form of white rice. Before the bran and germ are removed, the rice grains are soaked, steamed and dried. This imparts the grains with some of the nutrients provided by the bran and germ. Converted rice often contains extra B vitamins, iron and calcium.	Relatively flavorless	Fluffy, grains tend to stay separate	Off-white in color	Between one and two years in an airtight container
Instant Rice	Instant rice, also called precooked or minute rice, is a type of rice that has been fully cooked and then dehydrated before being packaged. This type of rice is quick to prepare.	Virtually flavorless	Slightly mushy	White in color	Between one and two years in an airtight container

RICE CLASSIFICATIONS

Rice is classified according to size. An unrelated grain called wild rice is often sold alongside regular rice.

Long-Grain Rice

Long-grain rice features rice grains that are four to five times as long as they are wide and most often comes in white and brown varieties, although other colors are available. When cooked, long-grain rice becomes light and the grains are generally easily separated. Flavorful basmati rice, often featured in East Indian cooking, is a popular form of long-grain rice.

Medium-Grain Rice

Medium-grain rice features rice grains that are two to three times as long as they are wide and is produced in both white and brown varieties. When cooked, medium-grain rice is more moist than long-grain rice, but not as sticky as short-grain varieties. Medium-grain rice is typically fluffy after being cooked, but begins to clump as it cools. Calrose rice is a popular variety of medium-grain rice.

Short-Grain Rice

Short-grain rice features rice grains that are almost round and comes in white and brown varieties. When cooked, short-grain rice becomes very moist. Due to its high starch content, the grains tend to stick together. Arborio rice is a popular variety of short-grain rice. You will often see short-grain rice used in sushi, risotto, paella and even some desserts.

Wild Rice

While it is not truly a rice, wild rice is a similar grain that comes from a North American marsh grass. Wild rice is dark brown or black in color, has a nutty flavor and a texture that is quite chewy. Wild rice must be thoroughly rinsed prior to cooking and can take as long as an hour to cook. Because it can be quite expensive, many recipes combine wild rice with long- or medium-grain varieties of rice.

Types of Pasta

Macaroni and Cheese, Fettuccini Alfredo, Lasagna– there's no doubt that pasta rates as one of our favorite foods.

Pasta is very simple, just a mixture of flour, water, salt and sometimes eggs formed into noodles. The wonder of pasta, however, is its versatility. It comes in hundreds of shapes, thicknesses and sizes, and can be prepared in a mind-boggling number of ways.

Certain pasta-and-sauce combinations have become standard. For example, pasta that needs to be twirled when eaten, like fettuccine, is often served with a thick sauce that sticks to the pasta. Thinner sauces are usually paired with tubular-shaped pasta, like penne, so the sauce can seep into the holes.

Dried pasta is great to have on hand because it keeps for a long time if stored in an airtight container. You can also buy whole wheat and brown rice pastas, which contain more fiber and therefore are more nutritious than the white version, which is made from highly processed flours.

Long Pasta

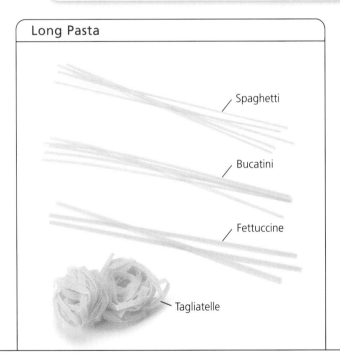

Spaghetti

Bucatini

Fettuccine

Tagliatelle

Tubular & Shaped Pasta

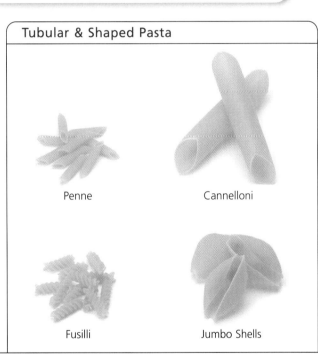

Penne

Cannelloni

Fusilli

Jumbo Shells

- Long round pastas, such as spaghetti, are usually served with sauces that stick to the strands, such as carbonara.

- Long hollow tubes, such as bucatini, are often served with tomato-based sauces.

- Long flat noodles, such as fettuccine, are excellent with creamy sauces, such as Alfredo.

- Pasta made with eggs, such as tagliatelle, are usually flat. Egg noodles often come in nests, which are pasta that is twisted into a coil shape before drying.

- Short pasta tubes, such as penne and macaroni, are often served with thick sauces or used in pasta casseroles.

- Larger tubes, such as cannelloni and manicotti, are often stuffed with meat or cheese mixtures and baked.

- Pastas are often named according to their shape. Some shaped pastas include fusilli (corkscrews) and orecchiette (little ears).

- Larger shaped pastas, such as jumbo shells (conchiglione), are often stuffed with meat or cheese mixtures and baked.

Tip

Is fresh pasta better than dried pasta?

It's a matter of preference. Aside from price, the only real difference between fresh and dried pasta is the texture. Fresh pasta tends to have a softer, less chewy texture than pasta that has been dried. Fresh pasta can be purchased at specialty pasta shops, the grocery store in the refrigerated section or made at home with a pasta maker.

Tip

What are Asian noodles?

Asian noodles have become popular in Western countries. With names like udon, soba and ramen, Asian noodles can be made from rice, buckwheat, mung beans or even seaweed. Instead of being paired with sauces, Asian noodles are often used as a base for meat, fish or vegetable dishes, as well as being a main ingredient in soups.

Pre-Stuffed Pasta

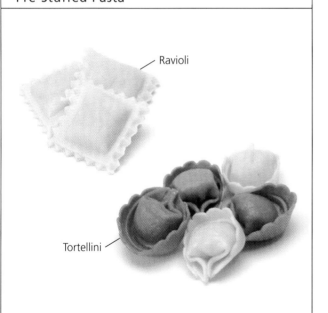

Ravioli

Tortellini

Grain-Like Pasta

Orzo

Couscous

- There are many types of pre-stuffed pastas available. Pre-stuffed pasta may be filled with meat, cheese, shellfish or vegetables.
- Pre-stuffed pasta can usually be purchased fresh or frozen.

- Pre-stuffed pastas are often served with a tomato or light, cream-based sauce.
- Examples of pre-stuffed pasta shapes include ravioli (square or round), agnolotti (half-moons) and tortellini (ring-shaped twists).

- Small, grain-like pastas are also popular. Some grain-like pastas, such as orzo, which looks like a grain of rice, are ideal in soups or served as a side dish.

- Couscous, which has a round barley shape, is also a type of pasta. Couscous is often featured in North African and Middle Eastern dishes as an accompaniment to stewed dishes or as a base for salads.

Types of Potatoes

Few foods are prepared in such a diverse number of ways as the potato. Mashed potatoes, French fries, roasted potatoes and many more dishes feature the noble spud. Fortunately, potatoes are a very healthy food.

The average potato contains only 100 calories and no sodium, fat or cholesterol. Potatoes also provide fiber, potassium and vitamin C.

SELECTING POTATOES
It's worth taking time to inspect the potatoes you intend to buy. Pick them up and feel them. The potatoes you select should be firm. Stay away from any that have a lot of wrinkles, blemishes or cracks, and do not buy potatoes that have sprouts or green areas, both of which contain a mildly toxic compound. If you are buying several potatoes that will be used whole in the same recipe, choose potatoes that are roughly the same size so they will cook evenly.

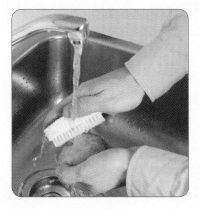

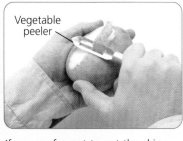

If you prefer not to eat the skin, you can easily remove it with a vegetable peeler or paring knife.

STORING POTATOES
The best place to keep potatoes is in a well-ventilated, dark location with a temperature between 45°F and 50°F. In these ideal conditions, your potatoes should last for several weeks. Potatoes stored at room temperature should be consumed within a week or two. You should not refrigerate potatoes or keep them in plastic bags.

PREPARING POTATOES
If you choose to eat the skin, which is packed with nutrients, make sure that you thoroughly scrub the outside of the potatoes before preparing and cooking them. Scrubbing should remove most of the remaining dirt and pesticides.

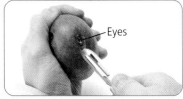

Any eyes (small, knobby sprouts) can also be removed with the tip of a vegetable peeler or paring knife.

POPULAR TYPES OF POTATOES

POTATO TYPE	DESCRIPTION	APPEARANCE	IDEAL FOR
Russet Potatoes	Also known as Idaho or baking potatoes, Russets are one of the most popular varieties of potato.	Oblong with rough, reddish-brown skin and white flesh	Baking, mashing, roasting and frying
White Potatoes	Available in round and long varieties. White potatoes hold their shape well when cooked and are a good general-purpose potato. Small white potatoes are called fingerling potatoes.	Round with smooth, light-tan skin and white flesh	Boiling, frying and baking
Red Potatoes	These attractively-colored potatoes hold together well when cooked and, with the skins on, make a bright addition to many dishes.	Round with smooth, red skin and white flesh	Steaming, roasting, boiling and pan-frying
New Potatoes	New potatoes are young, round potatoes that have been harvested before growing to full size.	Very small and round with thin light-tan or red skin and white flesh	Boiling, roasting whole and potato salads
Yellow Flesh Potatoes	Yellow flesh potatoes, such as the popular Yukon Gold variety, have a naturally sweet, buttery flavor.	Oval with light-tan skin and yellow flesh	Baking, roasting, mashing and frying
Sweet Potatoes	High in natural sugars and packed with nutrients, sweet potatoes are not actually potatoes but can be prepared in the same ways as ordinary potatoes. *Note: Sweet potatoes are often mistakenly referred to as yams, which are grown in tropical locations and differ in color, flavor and texture from sweet potatoes.*	Long and oval with reddish or orange skin and orange flesh	Boiling, baking, mashing and French-frying

Types of Vegetables

Packed with vitamins and minerals, vegetables are an essential part of a healthy diet and help add color and flavor to your meals. You can prepare vegetables in a wide variety of ways, and you should include at least one serving of vegetables in every meal.

Some vegetables, such as carrots, celery, garlic and onions, are staples that you should always have in your kitchen. Green onions and bell peppers are also useful to have on hand for adding flavor to dishes.

BUYING VEGETABLES

When choosing vegetables, freshness is the key. Look for vegetables with bright colors and crisp textures. If possible, find a reliable source of fresh vegetables, such as a local farmers' market. Buying vegetables in season is another way to ensure you find the freshest vegetables.

STORING VEGETABLES

Your vegetables will stay fresh longer if you store them dry and unwashed. Certain root vegetables, such as rutabagas, should be stored in a cool, dark place. Most other vegetables can be stored in the crisper drawer of your refrigerator.

CLEANING VEGETABLES

It is important to clean all your vegetables well, particularly those with edible skins. To clean most vegetables, thoroughly rinse them under cold running water or in a large bowl of water. If necessary, you can use a vegetable brush to remove surface dirt from vegetables that have firm surfaces, such as potatoes. After washing vegetables, you should remove any spoiled areas, since bacteria can thrive in these places.

If you are concerned about chemicals on the skins and inside your vegetables, you may want to consider purchasing organic vegetables, which are grown without pesticides. Keep in mind, though, that these vegetables must also be washed thoroughly.

COMMON TYPES OF VEGETABLES

CARROTS & PARSNIPS

Carrots and parsnips are packed with nutrients and are available year round. Carrots can be served either raw or cooked. When selecting carrots, consider purchasing bunches that still have the greens attached to ensure freshness.

Parsnips are similar to carrots, though they are never served raw. Look for crispness when choosing parsnips.

BROCCOLI & CAULIFLOWER

Broccoli and cauliflower can be enjoyed raw, steamed or boiled. Look for broccoli without any yellowing on the florets and white cauliflower that has tightly packed florets with no signs of browning.

RADISHES

With their signature peppery flavor and crunchy texture, raw radishes make a delicious addition to salads or vegetable platters. They can also be served cooked.

ASPARAGUS

Asparagus is most often prepared by boiling or steaming. You will find the freshest and most flavorful asparagus in the spring. Asparagus is available in green and white varieties.

CELERY

Celery is commonly enjoyed raw, either on its own or with fillings such as peanut butter or cream cheese. When cooked, celery is useful for flavoring foods such as soups and stews.

ZUCCHINI & CUCUMBER

Zucchini and cucumber are available year round. Zucchini can be enjoyed raw, sautéed, baked or grilled. Cucumbers are served raw and are often used in salads and sandwiches.

BELL PEPPERS

Bell peppers are available in a variety of colors, with the most common being green, yellow and red. Red and yellow peppers are more flavorful and more expensive than green bell peppers.

EGGPLANTS

Eggplants are never eaten raw, but are commonly baked, grilled or sautéed. When shopping, look for eggplants that have shiny, unbroken skins and a firm texture.

TOMATOES

Raw tomatoes are delicious in salads, while cooked tomatoes are commonly used in sauces. To find the freshest tomatoes, look for vine-ripened tomatoes at farmers' markets or grocery stores during the summer season.

AVOCADOS

Though avocados are high in calories, you can indulge in them knowing that they provide a healthy type of fat. Avocados are commonly enjoyed in guacamole dip or in salads. Ripe avocados will give a little when squeezed gently.

CORN

Corn is often boiled or grilled. You will most commonly find peaches and cream corn or yellow sweet corn. To test the freshness of a cob of corn, insert a fingernail into one of the kernels. If it squirts out a milky liquid, the corn is fresh.

PEAS

Common varieties of peas include the shell pea, snow pea and sugar snap pea. Shell peas must be removed from their pods. Snow peas and sugar snap peas can be eaten whole. Peas can be eaten raw, added to stir-fries, or enjoyed as side dishes.

BEANS

Common varieties of beans include green beans and wax beans. Beans are best when boiled or stir-fried until they are tender but still crisp. Green beans and wax beans are similar except for color, with wax beans being either yellow or purple.

TURNIPS & RUTABAGAS

Turnips and rutabagas can be found throughout the year. Though very similar, rutabagas are larger and taste sweeter than turnips. Both turnips and rutabagas are commonly prepared by roasting, boiling or stir-frying.

WINTER SQUASH

Common types of winter squash include acorn, butternut, spaghetti, Hubbard and buttercup squash. Winter squash is often prepared by roasting or steaming.

CABBAGES

As a source of vitamin C and fiber, cabbage is a nutritious addition to salads and stir-fries. You can find green and red varieties of cabbage, as well as Napa and Savoy cabbage.

Other members of the cabbage family include Brussels sprouts. Brussels sprouts resemble miniature cabbages and are often served as a boiled or steamed side dish.

MUSHROOMS

The most popular type of mushroom is the white, or button, mushroom, which can be enjoyed raw or cooked. Brown creminis and Portobellos are closely related to white mushrooms but are more flavorful. Exotic mushroom varieties include chanterelles, morels and truffles. Some mushroom types, such as shiitake and porcini, are also available dried.

KALE, COLLARD GREENS & CHARD

Kale, collard greens and chard are all extremely healthy leafy vegetables. These flavorful vegetables must be cooked, often by steaming or boiling, and then sautéed. These greens are a tasty addition to soups.

BEETS

The beet is a low-calorie root vegetable that is available year round and is relatively inexpensive. Commonly roasted, steamed or boiled, beets are packed with nutrients.

ONIONS

There are many different types of onions, such as sweet onions, yellow onions, Spanish onions, red onions, shallots and green onions. Leeks are like large green onions and are commonly served as side dishes or used in soups.

GARLIC

Garlic is an extremely healthy way to add flavor to dishes. A head of garlic contains numerous individual cloves. When choosing garlic, look for a firm texture, a tightly packed head and a full covering of papery skin.

Types of Salad Greens

Salads are no longer simple appetizers made with a head of iceberg lettuce and drowned in dressing. Today's salads are dishes with character thanks to the variety of salad greens now readily available. Salads can be served as an accompaniment to a meal or as a satisfying meal all by themselves.

Salad greens are typically a good source of a variety of nutrients, including vitamin C, folate, calcium and beta-carotene. In general, salad greens that are darker in color usually provide more vitamins and minerals. By including a large variety of greens in your salads, you are tossing in balanced nutrition and interesting flavors.

BUYING SALAD GREENS

Salad greens can be purchased in a number of forms. You can buy heads of lettuce, bunches of greens or even pre-washed and pre-mixed bags of salad greens.

Take the time to inspect your greens before buying them. Avoid any that are wilted, limp, browned or mushy.

STORING SALAD GREENS

In general, you should not wash greens before storing them. They should be stored in the fridge in their original packaging or a plastic bag that is not tightly sealed. Wrap bunched greens, such as watercress or arugula, in damp paper towels and place them in unsealed plastic bags in the fridge. Romaine lettuce, on the other hand, can be washed ahead of time and kept in the fridge in a vegetable storage bag.

CLEANING SALAD GREENS

To clean salad greens, immerse them in a bowl of lukewarm water. Gently move the greens through the water, allowing any dirt to fall to the bottom of the bowl. Then remove the greens from the bowl, rinse under running water, and dry in a salad spinner.

For greens that tend to be sandy, such as spinach, immerse the greens in fresh water as many times as necessary, emptying, rinsing and refilling the bowl of water until no sand remains.

TYPES OF LETTUCE

Boston & Bibb Lettuce 	Both Boston and Bibb lettuces have floppy, light-green leaves, loosely attached to the head. The leaves are soft with a mild, somewhat sweet flavor.	Iceberg Lettuce 	This traditional salad lettuce has crisp, light-green leaves that wrap tightly around the head. The flavor of the leaves is very mild.
Leaf Lettuce 	Leaf lettuce refers to several types of lettuce which grow loosely on stems rather than in heads. The colors of leaf lettuce can range from bright green to deep red and the texture of the leaves can be either smooth or ruffled. The flavor tends to be delicate and mild.	Romaine Lettuce 	This familiar lettuce is known for its long, green leaves which come tightly packed and joined on a stem. The crisp leaves can vary from deep green on the outside of the head to yellow green in the center, or heart. Romaine is the lettuce used to make Caesar salads.

OTHER TYPES OF SALAD GREENS

You can use any of these salad greens as an accent in a salad, or buy a mix called mesclun, which combines a variety of these greens.

Arugula 	This dark-green salad green has a flavor that is slightly bitter and peppery. Arugula works well when mixed with a mild-tasting lettuce or all on its own.	Radicchio 	Radicchio has magenta leaves that come on a tightly-formed head. It adds both pungent flavor and bright color to salads.
Belgian Endive 	Belgian endive comes in a tightly packed, pale yellow-and-white head that resembles a football. It's great in a salad or as a garnish.	Spinach 	This salad green has dark green leaves which can be oval and smooth in bunches of baby spinach or large and bumpy when fully grown.
Frisée 	This slightly bitter salad green has frilly, pale-yellow leaves. Frisée adds textural interest and flavor to mixed salads.	Watercress 	Watercress is known for its peppery flavor and leaves that are shaped like clover. It makes a nice addition to mild salads.

Types of Fruit

Fruits are an excellent way to add nutrients, delicious flavors and bright colors to your dishes.

BUYING FRUIT

It's an age-old problem: how to select ripe fruit at the store. Because many fruits are picked and shipped before they have ripened, finding fresh, ripe fruit is not a straightforward task. In general, you should look for fruit that feels heavy for its size and does not have any cuts, bruises or signs of mold.

Fruit that is in season in your region at the time you are shopping is most likely to be ripe. Try to find a local farmer's market where you can buy ripe fruit straight from the source. Another advantage of buying local fruit is that it will have been grown using pesticide regulations that are more stringent than those in some countries outside of the U.S. and Canada.

RIPENING FRUIT

If you do buy fruit that is not ripe, you can often speed up the ripening process at home with a paper bag. Place the fruit in a paper bag pierced with several pencil-sized holes and then loosely close the top of the bag. Allow the bag to sit on the counter at room temperature and check on the fruit each day to see if it has ripened. Once ripe, the fruit should be eaten or stored in the fridge to be eaten within a day or two.

CLEANING FRUIT

All fruit should be washed before they are eaten, peeled or cut. Even if you plan to peel or cut up fruit, you should still wash the fruit first. Bacteria on the outside of fruit can be transferred to the inside by a peeler or knife.

TREE FRUITS

Apples, pears, peaches, nectarines, plums and apricots are all examples of tree fruits. These fruits have skins that can be eaten.

Apples are generally ripe when picked and should be refrigerated immediately after purchase. Pears, peaches, nectarines, plums and apricots are often shipped before they are ripe and should be kept at room temperature until fully ripe. Once ripe, they should be stored in the refrigerator.

MELONS

There are many types of melons available. Cantaloupe, honeydew melons and watermelons are all popular examples. The skin, or rind, of a melon is not usually eaten so melons are normally peeled or cut into slices for eating. Ripe melons will give a bit if slightly pressed on the stem end. Give cantaloupes the sniff test—if they smell fragrant at the stem end, they are probably ripe and will taste sweet. Avoid melons that are very soft or have soft spots on them.

GRAPES, CHERRIES & BERRIES

Grapes, cherries and berries, such as blueberries, strawberries and raspberries, all have thin skins. These fruits are best consumed within 2 to 3 days of purchase.

CITRUS FRUIT

Lemons, limes, grapefruit and oranges are all citrus fruits. While the peels are not eaten with the fruit, the peel can be grated or zested and used as ingredients in various recipes. Citrus fruits will keep in the refrigerator for up to three weeks.

TROPICAL FRUITS

Tropical fruits like bananas, papayas, guavas, kiwi, pineapples and mangos usually have skins that are not eaten. These fruits should be kept at room temperature until they are ripe. Once ripe, tropical fruits can be refrigerated for several days. One exception is bananas, which should never be refrigerated.

About Eggs

Give your eggs a break today! Each year, Americans will enjoy about 270 eggs per person. You can test a raw egg for freshness by placing it in a glass of water. A fresh egg will sink to the bottom. An older egg will have lost some moisture, which is replaced with air, so an older egg will float on the surface. Egg washing and the application of a protective coating are part of the packaging process, so washing eggs before storing or cooking is not necessary.

As an alternative to traditional eggs, pasteurized liquid eggs can also be found in the refrigerated section of your local grocery store. This product, which can be egg whites, egg yolks, or a combination of the two, is pasteurized at a high heat that destroys bacteria without cooking the eggs.

About Eggs

Storing Eggs

* Eggs contain high amounts of vitamins and nutrients. Eggs also contain all nine amino acids, making eggs a complete protein.

* Egg yolk is a good source of protein, iron, calcium, vitamins A and D, phosphorus and choline.

* Egg white is a good source of protein and riboflavin.

* The average egg contains around 200 mg of cholesterol and about 70 calories. All of the cholesterol in an egg is contained in the yolk.

* Eggs should always be refrigerated because they are highly perishable at room temperature. Eggs left unrefrigerated for more than 2 hours should be discarded.

* Do not store eggs in the refrigerator door because this is the warmest place in the fridge and is not cold enough for storing eggs.

* Eggs will keep best if stored in their original carton.

* Eggs will last 4 to 5 weeks if properly refrigerated and should be used before the expiry date printed on the carton.

Tip *What tastes better: white eggs or brown eggs?*

Shell color does not affect the taste or nutritive quality of eggs—the breed of hen that laid the egg determines the egg's shell color. For instance, hens with white feathers and ear lobes lay white eggs, and hens with red feathers and ear lobes lay brown eggs. The yolk color is determined by the hen's diet. Hens that eat grass, alfalfa and yellow corn lay eggs with lighter yolks than wheat-fed hens.

Tip *Is it safe to eat raw or partially cooked eggs?*

Around 1 in 20,000 raw eggs will contain salmonella, a bacteria that causes food poisoning. Certain people, such as children, pregnant women, the elderly and people who have compromised immune systems should avoid eating raw or partially cooked eggs. To reduce your risk of salmonella poisoning, you may want to consider using pasteurized eggs.

Grade and Size

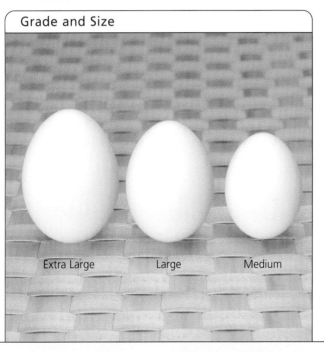

Extra Large   Large   Medium

Specialty Eggs

- Eggs are sold according to size, from "jumbo" down to "peewee." Sizes are determined by how much the average dozen weighs.

- Unless the recipe calls for a different size, use large eggs for cooking and baking.

- Eggs fall into one of three grades: AA, the highest quality, A, the second highest quality, and B, the lowest quality.

- Only AA and A grade eggs are widely available and, because there is very little difference between the two grades, less-expensive A grade eggs are a good choice.

- Specialty eggs are available in many grocery stores. They may be more expensive.

- Free-range eggs are eggs laid by hens that have been allowed to live outdoors. Some prefer these eggs because they feel the hens are treated more humanely.

- Organic eggs are eggs laid by hens that have been fed a diet free of drugs and hormones.

- Omega-3 eggs are eggs laid by hens that have been fed grains that contain high amounts of omega-3 fatty acids. These heart-healthy compounds are passed onto the eggs the hens produce.

About Poultry

Poultry can be prepared and served in countless ways. The most common types of poultry are chicken and turkey.

Free-range chickens and turkeys are birds that have been allowed time outdoors and are often grain-fed. Organic poultry is free-range, grain-fed poultry that is completely free of hormones and antibiotics.

PURCHASING POULTRY

You can purchase fresh, frozen or previously frozen poultry. A previously frozen bird has been frozen and then thawed for sale. Previously frozen poultry should not be refrozen before it is cooked.

When purchasing fresh poultry, look for birds that are moist and plump, without a strong odor.

The color of skin on a chicken can range from white to yellow, but you should avoid chicken with skin that looks transparent or blotchy. Turkey skin should always be cream-colored.

STORING POULTRY

You can store fresh, raw poultry in its original wrapping in the bottom of the refrigerator. To prevent leaks, wrap the package in plastic or aluminum foil. The poultry will keep this way for two or three days. You can keep whole birds in the freezer for up to 12 months, poultry pieces for up to 9 months and ground poultry for 3 to 4 months.

WHOLE POULTRY

Turkeys, chickens and game hens are commonly sold as whole birds.

Turkeys usually weigh between 8 and 24 pounds and are usually roasted.

Two types of chickens that are most commonly sold whole are roasters and broilers, or fryers. Roasters weigh 3 1/2 to 6 pounds and are usually served roasted, stewed or braised. Broilers, or fryers, weigh 2 to 5 pounds and are best when roasted, sautéed or fried.

Rock Cornish game hens weigh under 2 pounds and are perfectly sized for one person. These birds are often roasted, sautéed or braised.

When you purchase a whole bird, the giblets are generally packaged together and inserted in the cavity of a whole chicken. The giblets include the neck, heart, liver and gizzard.

POULTRY PARTS

You can purchase parts of chickens and turkeys. Parts are often available as bone-in, boneless, skin-on and skinless.

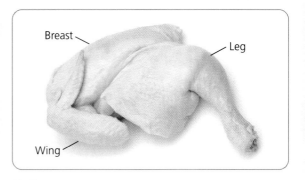

Cut Up

A cut up chicken is a whole chicken that has been cut into parts but sold packaged together.

Half

A half is one entire side of a chicken or turkey. A half contains one breast, one leg and one wing.

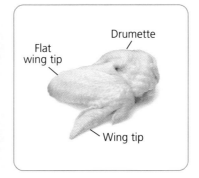

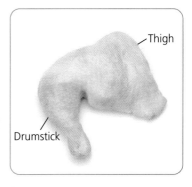

Breast

The breast is considered white meat and is one of the most popular poultry parts. Breast meat is very healthy and is low in fat, especially after the skin has been removed.

A breast is half of the entire chest area of a chicken or turkey. A double, or whole, breast, is both halves of the chest area with the center breast-bone still intact.

Wing

The wing contains a lot of bone and is considered white meat. There are three sections of a wing. The flat wing tip and drumette are closest to the body and contain the most meat. The wing tip is the outermost section of the wing and is often removed before sale.

Leg

The leg is made up of the thigh, or top part of the leg, and drumstick, or lower part of the leg. You can usually purchase the entire leg or just the thigh or drumstick separately. The leg is considered dark meat and has more fat content than white meat, but is more flavorful and does not dry out when overcooked, as does white meat.

About Beef

Before buying beef, you should know what type of beef to look for and understand a few key facts about the cuts of beef.

Beef is muscle tissue. A section, or cut, of beef may be made up of just one muscle or parts of several muscles plus some bone. The part of the cow that a cut comes from has a lot to do with the tenderness of the beef. Frequently-used muscles, such as those in the powerful hind quarter, will produce tougher beef than less-used muscles, such as those in the midsection.

The cut of beef you choose will help determine how you will prepare the beef.

CUTS OF BEEF

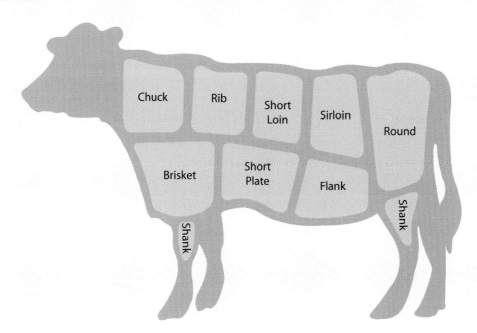

Tender Cuts
The rib, short loin and sirloin sections provide the most tender cuts of beef. Tender cuts of beef are usually best cooked using dry heat methods, such as sautéing, grilling, roasting, and frying. The rib cuts include delmonico or rib steaks and rib roasts. The short loin cuts provide the delectable porterhouse and T-bone steaks, tenderloin and filet mignon. The sirloin cuts include sirloin steaks.

Intermediate Cuts
The short plate and flank sections provide meat that is somewhat tough but has enough fat to help tenderize the meat naturally. Cuts of beef from these sections are ideal for cutting into strips and preparing for fajitas and stir-fries. The short plate cuts include skirt steaks, while the flank cuts include flank steak.

Tough Cuts
The toughest cuts of beef come from the chuck, brisket, round and shank sections. Tougher cuts of beef usually require slow, moist heat cooking methods, such as braising and stewing. The chuck cuts include shoulder and blade steaks and arm pot roasts. The brisket cuts are best for pot roasting. Round cuts include top and bottom round roasts and rump roasts.

MARBLING & AGING

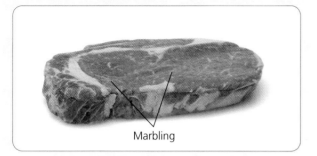

Marbling

Often, beef cuts contain streaks of fat interlaced throughout the meat. These streaks of fat, referred to as marbling, can add flavor and help tenderize the beef as it cooks. The more marbling a cut of beef has, the better.

Aged meat is available in high-end butcher shops and some supermarkets. Aged beef has been stored in a controlled environment for up to several weeks. This storage tenderizes the meat and intensifies the flavor of the beef.

BEEF GRADES

There are eight grading levels used to indicate the quality of beef.

- Prime is the highest quality beef. It has the most marbling and is flavorful and tender. Prime beef is usually only found in high-end butcher shops.
- Choice is normally the highest quality beef found in supermarkets. Choice beef has some marbling and is quite tender.
- Select beef has less marbling and is less tender than Prime or Choice, but is also less expensive.
- Standard and Commercial grades are not usually indicated on the packaging and are often sold as generic, or store-brand, beef.

There are also three lower grading levels, but beef of these lower grades is not sold to the public.

TIPS FOR BUYING & STORING BEEF

When you purchase beef, the meat should be firm, cold, moist, smell fresh and not look gray. Any fat on the edges of the meat should be creamy white. The packaging should be in good condition and should not contain much liquid.

Refrigerate fresh meat and use it within two days of purchase. You can freeze ground beef for up to three months or cuts of beef for up to six months.

SPECIAL TYPES OF BEEF

Angus Beef

Angus beef comes from the Angus breed of cattle and is considered high-quality beef. Some people feel that Angus beef is more tender and has better flavor than beef from other cow breeds.

Veal

Veal is meat from young male cows. Milk-fed veal means that the calves are fed a milk supplement which gives the meat a creamy pink color and fine texture. Grain-fed veal means that the calves are fed grain and hay, which gives the meat a darker color and more marbling than milk-fed veal.

About Pork

Before you head out to the grocery store to pick up some pork for dinner, take some time to educate yourself on the wide variety of pork available.

A section, or cut, of pork may be made up of just one muscle or parts of several muscles plus some bone. Frequently-used muscles, such as those in the legs and shoulders, will produce tougher pork than less-used muscles, such as those in the midsection.

Often, pork cuts contain streaks of fat interlaced throughout the meat. These streaks of fat, referred to as marbling, can add flavor and help tenderize the pork as it cooks. The more marbling a cut of pork has, the better.

FRESH, CURED & SMOKED PORK

There are many different types of pork to purchase, whether it is fresh, smoked or cured.

Fresh pork is meat that has not been cured or smoked. Cured pork, such as prosciutto, is meat that has been salted and then stored until the salt has penetrated the meat. Smoked pork, such as ham, is meat that has been cured and then smoked to give the meat an extra smoky flavor.

TIPS FOR BUYING & STORING PORK

Pork that you purchase should be pink, firm and moist, while any fat on the edges should be creamy white. The packaging should be cold and in good condition.

Refrigerate fresh pork and use it within two days of purchase. You can freeze ground pork for up to three months or cuts of pork for up to six months.

CUTS OF PORK

The cut of pork you choose will help determine how you should prepare the pork. No matter what method you choose to prepare your pork, make sure it is cooked to an internal temperature of 160°F to ensure any harmful bacteria are eliminated.

Loin
Cuts

Leg
Cuts

Shoulder
Cuts

Side
Cuts

Shoulder Cuts

Pork shoulder cuts are somewhat fatty, which provides the cuts with lots of flavor. These economical cuts are often best cooked using slow, moist heat cooking methods, such as braising and stewing. Shoulder cuts are often also used for making sausage and ground pork. Examples of shoulder cuts include blade roasts and steaks, picnic roasts and hocks.

Side Cuts

Pork side cuts are tender, flavorful and contain a considerable amount of fat. Cuts from this area are usually best cooked using dry heat methods, such as sautéing, grilling, roasting, and frying. Popular examples of side cuts include spareribs, bacon and brisket.

Loin Cuts

The loin section provides the leanest and most tender cuts of pork. Tender cuts are usually best cooked using dry heat methods, such as sautéing, grilling, roasting and frying. Many loin cuts are available either boneless or bone-in. Examples of popular loin cuts include tenderloin, loin chops, back ribs and sirloin roasts.

Leg Cuts

The leg section, consisting of the rump and back legs, provides lean, flavorful cuts that are not as tender, and often more economical, than loin cuts. Leg cuts are usually best cooked using slow, moist heat cooking methods, such as braising and stewing. Leg cuts can be purchased boneless or bone-in and are often either cured or smoked. Popular examples of leg cuts include ham roasts and steaks as well as leg cutlets.

About Fish

If you're looking for nutrition and variety, fish and shellfish are excellent choices, especially for a low-fat diet. While all fish are not created equal, most types of fish are low in fat, cholesterol and calories and contain oodles of protein, vitamin B and omega-3 fatty acids. Crustaceans, such as lobster or shrimp, are good sources of calcium, iron and other minerals.

The fish you see in stores may be farm-raised or wild and are often sold as fillets or steaks. Fillets are meaty, boned cuts of fish available with or without the skin. Steaks are pieces cut widthwise from the whole fish and most often include a central bone. Salmon, halibut and swordfish are the fish most commonly sold as steaks.

You should refrigerate fresh fish in the original wrapper and serve it within a day or two of purchase.

Fish

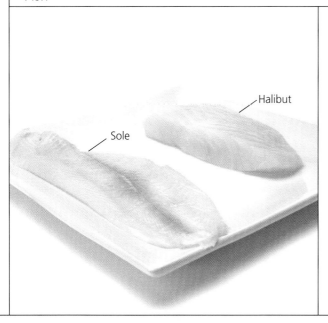

Halibut

Sole

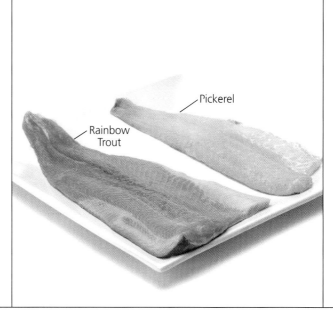

Pickerel

Rainbow Trout

Flat Fish

- Flat fish are thin, oval-shaped fish and have both eyes on top.

- Examples of flat fish include sole, halibut, flounder, fluke and plaice.

- Most flat fish have light-colored, mild-tasting flesh.

- Each flat fish provides 4 fillets.

Round Fish

- Round fish are fish that have a tube-shaped body. Round fish also have one eye on each side of the head.

- Examples of round fish include rainbow trout, pickerel, bass, perch, red snapper and salmon.

- The flavor and color of the flesh depends on the type of fish.

- Each round fish provides 2 fillets.

Tip

Can I also purchase whole fish?

Yes. You can purchase pan-dressed fish, which are whole fish that have had the innards, scales, head, tail and fins removed. Drawn fish are whole fish that have had the innards and scales removed, but have the head, tail and fins still attached. You can even purchase a whole fish just the way it comes from the water and remove the innards and scales yourself.

Tip

What should I look for when buying fish?

The fish flesh should be firm, with no browning or strong fishy odor. Feel free to ask to smell the fish before purchasing. Check whole fish to make sure that the skin is shiny, the eyes are clear and slightly protruding and the gills are bright red and not slimy.

Shellfish

Lobster

Shrimp

Mussels

Oysters

Clams

Crustaceans

- Crustaceans are a type of shellfish that have a segmented body with an outer shell, a tail, small legs and usually two claws.

- Examples of crustaceans include shrimp, lobster, crab and crayfish.

- Crustaceans usually have a heartier flavor and texture than fish.

- Live crustaceans you purchase should move their claws when they are touched.

Mollusks

- Mollusks are a type of shellfish that have a one or two-piece hard shell surrounding a soft body.

- Examples of mollusks with a one-piece shell include snails and squid. Mollusks with a two-piece shell include clams, oysters and mussels.

- Mollusks you purchase should be alive and have a closed shell. To test whether a mollusk with an open shell is alive, tap it gently. A live mollusk will close its shell when tapped.

Techniques

Learning the right way to perform everyday tasks will make your work in the kitchen much more easy, efficient and enjoyable. From chopping and marinating to steaming and roasting, this section will show you the best techniques for preparing foods. You will also learn cooking techniques you will use in the kitchen on a regular basis.

3 Food Preparation Techniques

Slicing

Dicing

Chopping

Creating Julienne Cuts

Pounding Meat

Breading

Marinating

Whipping

4 Preparing Specific Foods

Peel & Seed a Tomato

Dice & Mince Onions

Prepare Leeks

Peel & Mince Garlic

Cut & Seed Bell Peppers

Clean & Slice Mushrooms

Prepare Broccoli

Seed & Peel Avocados

Prepare Melons

Prepare Apples, Pears & Strawberries

Zest & Grate Citrus Fruit

Juice Citrus Fruits

Break & Separate Eggs

Beat & Fold in Egg Whites

Cook & Peel Hard-Cooked Eggs

Working With Fresh Herbs

5 Cooking Techniques

Stovetop Basics

Simmering

Poaching

Boiling, Parboiling & Blanching

Steaming

Sweating Vegetables

Cooking Vegetables

Cooking Pasta

Deep Frying & Shallow Frying

Sautéing, Pan Frying & Stir-Frying

Reducing

Searing

Deglazing

Stewing & Braising

Roasting

Baking Tips

Slicing

Slicing is the process of cutting foods into flat pieces of the same thickness, such as potatoes for potato chips, zucchinis for grilling, tomatoes for sandwiches and pineapples for serving. Slicing is the basis for many other cuts, including dicing (see page 71), chopping (see page 72) and julienne (see page 73).

Once you have the hang of slicing foods evenly, cutting up vegetables for everything from stir-fries to vegetable soups will be a breeze.

When slicing food, the cuts should be evenly spaced and parallel to one another in order to ensure consistency in the thickness of the slices. This consistency will help ensure the food cooks evenly.

Slicing

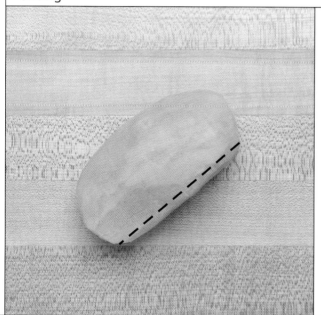

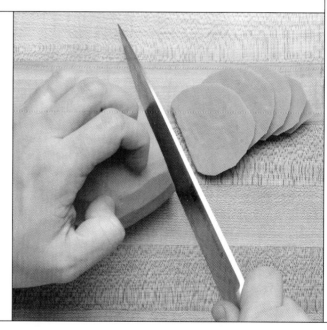

- Slicing is the process of cutting foods into flat pieces of the same thickness.

- In the photos, a peeled sweet potato is used to demonstrate slicing.

1 To create a flat surface to make the item easier and more stable to work with, cut a lengthwise slice close to the outer edge of the item. Then place the item cut side down on a cutting board.

2 Make evenly spaced lengthwise or widthwise cuts to create slices.

- In the photo, the cuts are 1/4 inch apart. You can change the thickness of your slices by making your cuts wider or narrower.

Dicing

When you dice, you cut ingredients into cubes that are the same size on all sides. Dice ranges in size from 1/4 to 3/4 inch cubes. Recipes that call for dice include salsas, soups, stews and cheese platters. Since dicing produces cubes that are consistent in size, diced ingredients cook evenly in dishes.

To create dice, you begin by making a lengthwise slice close to the item's outside edge to create a flat side large enough to keep the item stable while cutting. To create large dice, make parallel cuts three-quarters of an inch apart. To create small dice, make parallel cuts one-quarter of an inch apart. Remember, be precise and make sure your cutting hand is steady to produce dice that is consistent in size.

Dicing

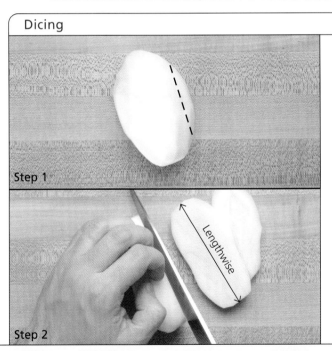

Step 1

Step 2

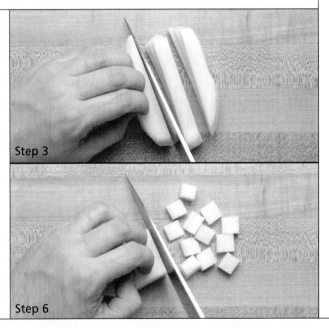

Step 3

Step 6

- Dicing is the process of cutting food into cubes the same size on each side. In this example, we cut 1/2 inch dice.

1 To create a flat surface to make the item easier and more stable to work with, cut a lengthwise slice close to the item's outside edge and place the item cut side down on a cutting board.

2 Make lengthwise cuts 1/2 of an inch apart to create slices. Keep the slices together in the order they were cut.

3 Stack and line up the edges of 3 or 4 slices. Holding the stack with one hand, make lengthwise cuts 1/2 of an inch apart to create sticks.

4 Repeat step 3 for the remaining slices.

5 Position the sticks in stacks of 3 or 4. Gather 3 or 4 stacks together and line up the edges.

6 Holding the stacks with one hand, make widthwise cuts 1/2 of an inch apart to create dice.

7 Repeat steps 5 to 6 to cut the remaining sticks into dice.

Chopping

You won't get very far in cooking if you don't know how to chop. Fortunately, chopping is a simple process that requires little precision. From meats and herbs to vegetables and nuts, you can put just about any food down on the cutting board and cut it up into pieces of roughly the same size. What could be easier?

If your recipe calls for an item to be finely chopped, it means that the final pieces should be tiny—roughly the size of a sunflower seed or smaller. If the recipe calls for an ingredient to be coarsely chopped, you simply cut it into big chunks—approximately the width of a large ice cube. To adjust the size of your pieces, you simply change the width and number of cuts you make.

Fine Chopping

Coarse Chopping

- Fine chopping, sometimes called mincing, is the process of cutting food into small pieces of less than 1/4 of an inch.

- In the photo, a clove of garlic is used to illustrate fine chopping.

- While almost any food can be finely chopped, items like herbs, nuts and garlic are often finely chopped.

- To finely chop an item, you cut it into thin pieces and then cut across the pieces to create smaller pieces. You can further chop the pieces to make them even smaller.

- Coarse chopping, sometimes called rough chopping, is the process of cutting food into large pieces of more than 3/4 of an inch.

- In the photo, a potato is used to illustrate coarse chopping.

- Almost any medium- or large-sized item can be coarsely chopped. Items such as carrots and celery are often coarsely chopped.

- To coarsely chop an item, you simply cut it into large chunks. It is not important for the pieces to be exactly the same size or shape.

Creating Julienne Cuts

Creating julienne cuts is a skill that will take some time and effort to perfect. When you julienne a food item, you cut it into short, matchstick-sized strips. Julienne-cut foods are often used as garnishes or salad toppings.

Requiring a steady hand and a bit of precision, julienne-cut foods measure 1/8 inch high by 1/8 inch wide. The length of the julienne cuts will depend on the recipe in which they will be used. With practice, you will be able to create even, parallel cuts that produce strips that are consistent in size. You should be aiming for strips that resemble matchsticks. It may also be helpful to think of french fries as oversized julienne-cut potatoes.

Creating Julienne Cuts

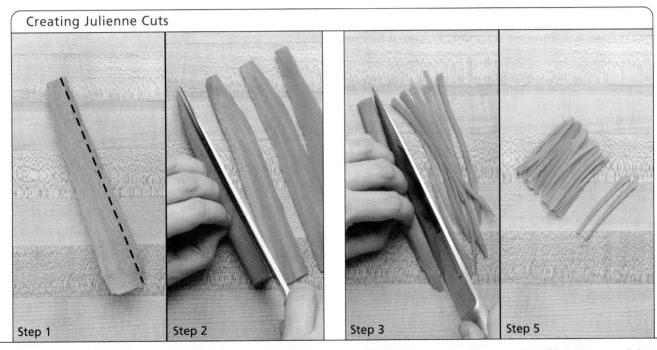

Step 1 **Step 2** **Step 3** **Step 5**

- When you julienne an item, you cut it into short, matchstick-sized strips.
- In the photo, a peeled carrot is used to demonstrate creating julienne cuts.

1 To create a flat surface to make the item easier and more stable to work with, cut a lengthwise slice close to the outer edge of the item and place the item cut side down on a cutting board.

2 Make lengthwise cuts 1/8 of an inch apart to create slices. Keep the slices together in the order they were cut.

3 Stack and line up the edges of 3 or 4 slices. Holding the stack with one hand, make lengthwise cuts 1/8 of an inch apart to create julienne cuts.

4 Repeat step 3 for the remaining slices.

Note: Slices that are rounded on one side do not stack well and should be cut individually, cut side down.

5 Gather the julienne sticks, line up the edges and cut into the desired length.

Pounding Meat

Pounding is a technique in which you hammer cuts of meat into a flat, even thickness. The benefit of pounding meat is that it helps to cook the meat evenly and can sometimes increase its tenderness.

Heavy, hammer-like tools called meat tenderizers (also called meat mallets or meat pounders) are normally used to pound meat. Typically made of metal or wood, they usually have two surfaces—one flat and one textured. Always use the flat side as the textured side will tear the meat.

Pounding is often used to flatten boneless chicken breasts and thick slices of beef or pork. When pounding, you should always wrap the meat in plastic wrap and work from the middle of the meat outward. Avoid the edges to keep them from becoming too thin and ragged.

Pounding Meat

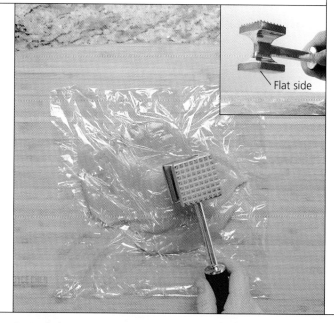

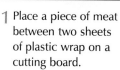

Flat side

- Pounding is a process that flattens pieces of meat into an even thickness so the meat becomes slightly more tender and will cook quickly and evenly.

- A boneless chicken breast is shown in the photos to demonstrate pounding.

1 Place a piece of meat between two sheets of plastic wrap on a cutting board.

2 Firmly hammer the middle of the piece of meat with the flat side of a meat tenderizer. Continue hammering the meat, moving outwards from the middle, until the entire piece of meat is the desired thickness.

- If you do not have a meat tenderizer, you can pound meat with a rolling pin or the bottom of a heavy saucepan.

Breading

If it has a nice crispy crust, the food you just bit into may have been breaded. Breading is a process that coats food in a mixture that turns into a crunchy crust. Breading is commonly used in dishes like chicken parmigian and pork schnitzel.

When breading an item, you usually dip the food item into three mixtures: a flour mixture typically containing salt, pepper and sometimes other seasonings, an egg-and-water mixture and a dry breading mixture which becomes the crust. Items such as bread crumbs, cornmeal, cracker crumbs and chopped nuts can be used in the dry breading mixture.

To properly bread an item, you will need three containers large enough to hold the largest piece of food—pie plates or other baking pans make an excellent choice. You'll also need a tray or plate large enough to hold all of the breaded items in a single layer afterward.

Breading

Step 1 — Seasoned Flour / Egg Wash / Dry Breading Mixture

Step 2

Step 3

Step 4

- In the photos, a chicken breast is used to demonstrate breading.

1 Set up 3 containers in a row. The first should contain seasoned flour (such as 1/2 cup flour, 1 tsp salt and 1/4 tsp pepper combined), the second an egg wash (1 egg and 2 tsp water beaten together) and the third a dry breading mixture of your choice.

2 Place the item in the seasoned flour and then turn it over to make sure all sides are coated. Lift the item and shake off any excess seasoned flour.

3 Dip the item in the egg wash, making sure all sides are coated. Lift the item and allow the excess to drip off.

4 Place the item in the breading mixture and pile a handful of the breading mixture on top so it is completely covered. Press down on the item to make sure the mixture adheres.

5 Lift the item and gently shake off any excess breading mixture.

6 Set the item down on a plate.

- Repeat steps 2 to 6 for the remaining items.

Marinating

Marinating is the process of soaking food in a liquid before cooking to give the food more flavor.

Most meat and poultry can be marinated anywhere from four hours to overnight. When marinating fish, be sure to follow the recipe closely, since leaving fish in a marinade for too long will affect the texture of the fish.

Resealable plastic bags are ideal for holding marinating foods, but you can also use a glass, stainless steel or ceramic bowl that is small enough to allow the food to be submerged in the marinade.

When working with marinades, you should always be cautious about bacteria. Be sure to store marinating food in the fridge and dispose of any leftover marinades immediately.

About Marinades

- A marinade is a liquid that foods like meat, poultry, seafood and vegetables are soaked in before they are cooked to give them more flavor.

- There are many types of marinades, but most contain some type of acidic ingredient such as vinegar, citrus juice, yogurt, buttermilk or wine.

- Along with the acidic ingredient, items such as salt, herbs, spices, oil and sugar are commonly added to give the food even more flavor.

How to Marinate

1 Place the item(s) you want to marinate in a resealable plastic bag with the marinade. Squeeze the air out of the bag, seal the top and squish the marinade around so that it evenly coats the food.

2 Place the bag on a plate or pan in the refrigerator to marinate. Turn the bag occasionally while the food is marinating.

3 When you are ready to cook, remove the item from the marinade.

Whipping

Whipping foods adds tiny air bubbles that increase the size, lighten the density and change the appearance and texture of foods. Whipped foods are light and fluffy.

Recipes generally call for ingredients that have been whipped until either the "soft peaks" or "stiff peaks" stage. To check this, lift the whisk out of the whipped mixture several times to form mounds. Smooth, pointed mounds that droop slightly are soft peaks. To obtain stiff peaks, continue whipping until you can form firm, pointed mounds. It is always best to under-whip than to over-whip.

Is there a difference between whipping and beating? Not really. Both techniques use the same process and the two terms are often used interchangeably. Technically though, ingredients such as eggs and batters are beaten to smooth and combine them, while ingredients such as egg whites and cream are whipped to incorporate air and make them fluffy. For information on beating egg whites, see page 94.

Whipping by Hand

Whipping with an Electric Mixer

Electronic hand mixer

- In the photos, heavy cream is used to demonstrate whipping.

- Whipping by hand involves rapidly mixing ingredients with a utensil, such as a large balloon whisk or wooden spoon.

- To whip ingredients by hand, tilt the bowl toward you slightly and stir the ingredients very rapidly so the utensil continually breaks the surface and adds air to the mixture.

- Whipping by hand requires a lot of effort. It takes roughly 100 stirs by hand to equal 1 minute of whipping with an electric mixer.

- You can also whip ingredients with an electric hand mixer or a stand mixer with a whisk attachment.

  Note: For information on the different types of mixers, see page 25.

- Whipping ingredients with a mixer is much easier, but you must be careful not to over-whip the ingredients.

- When whipping ingredients with an electric mixer, you should use one of the mixer's higher settings.

Peel & Seed a Tomato

While some recipes that include tomatoes require simply dicing or chopping, often you'll need to peel and seed your tomatoes before using them. Tomatoes are great in salads as is, but it's best to remove the skin and seeds when using tomatoes in sauces, purees, soups or canning. The skin and seeds can actually alter the texture and flavor of these foods. There are also times when you might want to seed a tomato but keep the peel on, as is commonly done before roasting.

In the steps below, you cut a shallow **X** at the bottom of the tomato so the skin will separate at this point when the tomato is placed in boiling water. This gives you a place to start peeling.

Peel a Tomato

Step 1

Step 2

Step 3

Step 4

- The best way to peel a tomato is to immerse it in boiling water for a short period of time to loosen the skin.

1 Bring a medium saucepan half-filled with water to a rapid boil with the lid on. Fill a large bowl half-way with cold water and several ice cubes.

2 Holding the tomato in one hand, remove the core and stem using a paring knife.

- The tough core of a tomato should be removed before the tomato is used in any recipe.

3 Cut a shallow **X** in the bottom of the tomato, slicing just through the skin.

4 Remove the lid from the pot of boiling water. Using a slotted spoon or tongs, carefully lower the tomato into the boiling water.

5 Leave the tomato in the boiling water for 20 to 30 seconds, depending on the size of the tomato.

Tip

Are canned tomatoes an acceptable substitute for fresh tomatoes?

Canned tomatoes are usually a great substitute for fresh tomatoes, especially when making foods such as sauces and stews. Canned tomatoes are very flavorful and can sometimes be a better option than fresh tomatoes that are not in season.

Tip

How can I quickly ripen a tomato?

If your tomatoes aren't quite ripe, you can help them along by placing them in a brown paper bag pierced with several pencil-sized holes for a day or two. The paper bag traps the ripening gases so the tomatoes can ripen faster. Also, remember to never refrigerate tomatoes as they will lose some of their flavor when chilled.

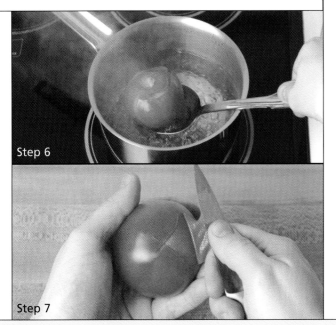

Step 6

Step 7

Seed a Tomato

Step 1

Step 2

6 Using the slotted spoon or tongs, remove the tomato from the boiling water and place it in the bowl of ice water for 1 minute.

7 Once the tomato has cooled, remove it from the cold water and dry the tomato with a paper towel. Using a paring knife, begin peeling the tomato at the **X** you cut in step 3.

• If the skin is still difficult to remove, repeat steps 4 through 7.

• You can seed a tomato with or without the peel intact.

1 Using a knife, cut the tomato in half widthwise

Note: For plum tomatoes, cut the tomato in half lengthwise.

2 Gently squeeze a tomato half over a bowl to remove the seeds. Any remaining seeds can be scooped out with your fingers or a small spoon. Repeat with the other tomato half.

Dice & Mince Onions

The difference between dicing and mincing lies in the size of the pieces. Minced pieces are cut smaller than diced pieces. Diced pieces can roughly range from the size of corn kernels to the size of sugar cubes, whereas minced pieces are roughly the size of sesame seeds.

When cutting an onion, keeping the root end intact allows you to easily dice the onion—holding it together while you cut.

To avoid teary eyes, chill onions for an hour in the fridge or for 10 minutes in the freezer before chopping. If you have leftover chopped onions, refrigerate them in a glass or stainless steel bowl covered with plastic for up to three days.

Dice an Onion

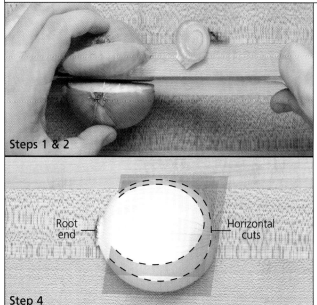

Steps 1 & 2

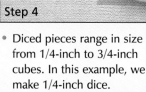

Root end — Horizontal cuts

Step 4

Lengthwise cuts

Widthwise cuts

Step 5

Step 6

Diced

Minced

- Diced pieces range in size from 1/4-inch to 3/4-inch cubes. In this example, we make 1/4-inch dice.

1 To dice an onion, lay the onion on its side and slice off the top. Do not slice off the root end.

2 Cut the onion in half lengthwise.

3 Remove the papery skin and any brown or spotted layers. Lay each onion half on a cutting board, cut side down.

4 Using your knife, make 2 horizontal cuts to within 1/2 inch of the root end.

5 Make several lengthwise cuts down through the onion, about 1/4 inch apart, without cutting through the root end.

6 Make several widthwise cuts down through the onion, about 1/4 inch apart, until you reach the root end. Discard the root end.

7 Repeat steps 4 to 6 with the other onion half.

- To make larger dice, make wider cuts in steps 5 and 6.

Mince an Onion

- To mince an onion, make narrower cuts in steps 5 and 6.

Prepare Leeks

Leeks are long, narrow members of the onion family. They have a mild flavor that is similar to that of ordinary onions. Leeks can be sliced and served raw as a salad topping or used to create a subtly flavored leek-and-potato soup.

The dark green tops of leeks are not edible and are cut off prior to washing. Leeks must be thoroughly cleaned before using them in a recipe due to the fact that they usually have a fair amount of soil hidden between their layers. For information on cooking leeks, see page 109.

Cleaned leeks can be wrapped in damp paper towels and stored in a plastic bag in the fridge for two days.

Prepare a Leek

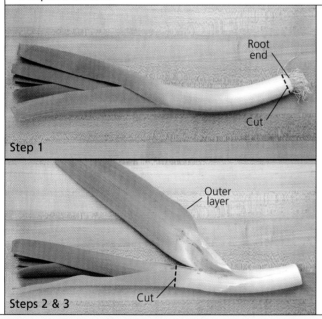

Step 1

Steps 2 & 3

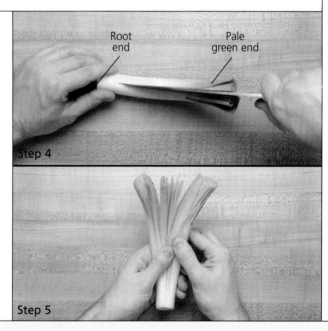

Step 4

Step 5

- Leeks are made up of many layers, much like onions. These layers often contain sand which must be rinsed away.

1 Place the leek on a cutting board. Cut 1/4 inch off the root end.

2 Peel off the outer layer and cut away any discolored layers of the leek.

3 Cut off the dark green leaves, leaving 2 inches of pale green along with the white portion of the leek.

4 Starting 1 inch in from the root end of the leek, slice through the center of the leek lengthwise toward and through the pale green end.

- The root end is left intact so the leek will not fall apart when you rinse it.

5 Fan out the leaves and rinse thoroughly between each layer with cold, running water.

6 Shake the leek over the sink and then pat it dry with a paper towel.

Peel & Mince Garlic

If you want to bring out the garlic flavor in your dish, you need to cut garlic, instead of leaving it whole. The more you cut garlic, the more pronounced the flavor becomes as it allows more oil from the garlic to be released.

Mincing involves cutting an ingredient into tiny pieces. Before you cut or mince garlic, you need to peel each garlic clove. If garlic pieces get stuck to the knife while mincing, carefully push the pieces down the side of the blade and off the sharp edge with your index finger.

You should never store peeled or minced garlic in a jar of oil for more than a day, as this can cause a serious form of food-poisoning called botulism. However, store-bought minced garlic in a jar is safe to use as it contains preservatives.

Peel a Garlic Clove

Step 1

Step 2

1 Separate a clove of garlic from the bulb, remove any excess papery skin and place the garlic clove on a cutting board.

2 Place the flat side of a chef's knife on top of the garlic clove and, using the heel of your hand, firmly press down on the blade until you hear a cracking sound.

3 Peel away the papery skin from the garlic clove.

4 Trim off the root end and any brown spots of the garlic clove.

Mince a Garlic Clove

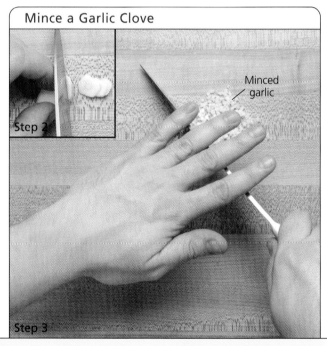

Step 2

Step 3

Minced garlic

1 Place a peeled garlic clove on a cutting board.

2 Using a chef's knife, make thin slices widthwise across the garlic clove.

3 Holding the handle of the knife in one hand, spread the fingers of your other hand on top of the blade, along the blunt back edge. Moving the handle up and down, gently rock the sharp edge of the blade on the cutting board and finely chop the garlic slices into tiny pieces.

Cut & Seed Bell Peppers

Red, yellow and orange peppers are green peppers that have been vine-ripened, allowing them to develop their sweetness and color. You can roast or grill red, yellow, orange and green peppers whole or use them chopped on top of pizza, sliced for serving with dips, or cut and tossed into a salad.

Before chopping or slicing a bell pepper, you'll need to remove the stem and core. Then make sure you always cut your cored peppers skin side down. If you like your peppers not just "red," but "red hot," you can prepare a hot pepper, such as a jalapeno, using a similar method as a bell pepper. Wash the hot pepper and cut off the top, leaving the bottom intact. Slice it in half lengthwise and scrape out the membrane and seeds, which contain most of the heat, with a teaspoon. To avoid accidentally irritating your eyes, wash your hands thoroughly with soap immediately after handling hot peppers.

Cut & Seed a Bell Pepper

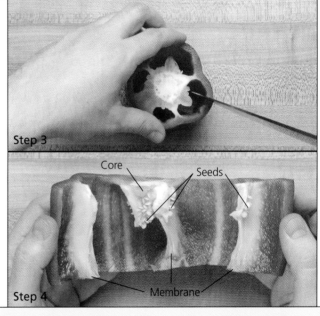

Step 3

Core   Seeds

Membrane

Step 4

- The stem, core and seeds of a bell pepper must be removed before it can be cut up.

1 Wash the pepper. Pat dry with a paper towel.

2 Place the pepper on its side on a cutting board and cut off the top and bottom of the pepper.

- The top and bottom pieces of the pepper are usable. Simply remove the stem and any remaining white membrane and seeds with a paring knife.

3 Make a lengthwise cut through the side of the pepper.

4 Gently pull the pepper apart at the cut. Remove the core and unroll the pepper on the cutting board, skin side down, to flatten.

5 Use a paring knife to cut out the white membrane and seeds.

- You can now chop or slice the pepper.

Clean & Slice Mushrooms

Including mushrooms in your recipes is a simple way to add flavor and texture to dishes such as sauces, salads, meat dishes and omelets. Cream of mushroom soup, stuffed mushrooms and stir-fries are some other delicious dishes that contain mushrooms.

Mushrooms can be eaten cooked or raw; whole, diced or sliced. Keep in mind that cut mushrooms brown easily, so wait until just before serving to cut mushrooms for uncooked dishes. You can eat the stems of most mushrooms, but some mushrooms, such as shiitakes, have inedible stems that should be discarded.

You can refrigerate your cleaned mushrooms in a bowl covered with a damp paper towel for one day.

Clean Mushrooms

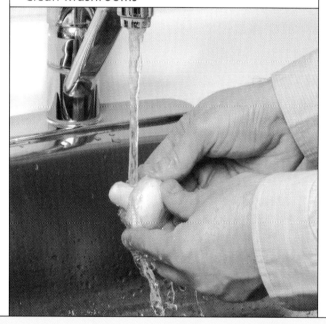

Slice a Mushroom

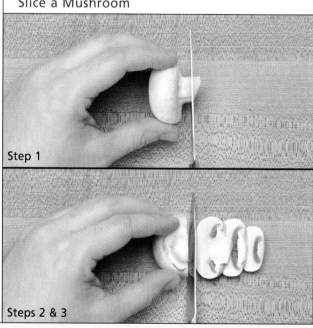

Step 1

Steps 2 & 3

- Mushrooms are often covered with dirt that must be cleaned off before cooking.

1 Lightly rinse each mushroom under cold running water. Use your fingers to gently rub off any stubborn dirt.

2 Place the mushrooms on a paper towel on the counter and gently blot the mushrooms dry with another paper towel.

1 Using a paring knife, cut off the bottom of the stem.

2 Place the mushroom on a cutting board, cap side down.

3 Slice the mushroom into pieces that are 1/4 of an inch thick or the size specified by the recipe.

Prepare Broccoli

Broccoli is packed with nutrients and flavor and is easy to prepare. When preparing broccoli, you will need to cut the florets from the main stem. To prepare broccoli for sautés and stir-fries, cut the florets from the stalk close to the florets. Larger florets can be cut in half, starting from the stem end, to ensure even cooking. To prepare broccoli for steaming, cut close to the main stalk, keeping several florets together.

After cutting away the florets, peel the leftover stalk, slice it thinly on the diagonal and cook it along with the rest of the broccoli. Sliced broccoli stalks are great in stir-fries and soups.

If you intend to serve broccoli raw, consider boiling it for just a few seconds and then plunging it into ice water to help bring out its vivid color and flavor. For more information, see Blanching on page 104.

Cleaning Broccoli

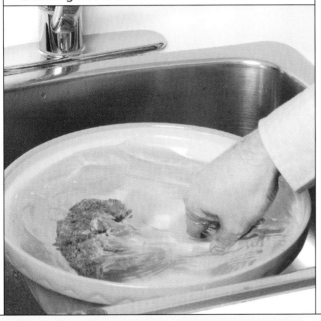

Cutting Broccoli

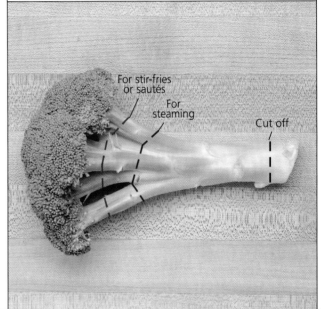

For stir-fries or sautés

For steaming

Cut off

1 Place a large bowl in the sink and fill the bowl with lukewarm water.

2 Immerse the broccoli in the water. Gently move the broccoli through the water, allowing any dirt to fall to the bottom of the bowl.

3 Remove the broccoli from the water and place it in a colander to drain.

4 Empty the bowl and rinse away any dirt on the bottom of the bowl.

5 If necessary, repeat steps 1 to 4 until the broccoli is clean.

1 Place the broccoli on a cutting board. Using a chef's knife, cut off the bottom half inch of the broccoli stalk.

2 Cut to separate the florets from the main stalk. For stir-fries and sautés, cut close to the florets. For steaming, cut close to the main stalk.

3 If you plan to cook the leftover stalk, use a vegetable peeler to remove the outer surface of the stalk. Then cut the stalk diagonally into 1/4-inch slices.

Seed & Peel Avocados

Many people are discovering the benefits of avocados, which are packed with nutrients, including folate, potassium, vitamins and heart-healthy fats.

A ripe avocado has a hard skin covering very soft, delicate flesh inside. Avocados are served raw, sliced in salads or mashed in guacamole and salad dressings. You can even add interest to a shrimp salad by serving it in seeded and peeled avocado halves.

Cut avocado browns easily. To help prevent discoloration, brush avocado pieces with lemon juice. You can also leave the pit and peel on unused avocado portions before covering with plastic wrap and refrigerating. When storing mashed or puréed avocado, cover it with plastic wrap that touches the surface of the avocado. If you do happen to have a discolored avocado, simply scrape off the brown areas of the fruit to reveal the flesh underneath.

Seed & Peel Avocados

Steps 1 & 2

Step 3

Step 4

Steps 5 & 6

1 Using a chef's knife, slice deeply around the length of the avocado. There is a large, hard seed in the middle of the avocado that will keep your knife from cutting all the way through.

2 Grasping both halves, gently twist them in opposite directions until they separate. Set down the halves on a cutting board.

3 Lightly strike the sharp edge of your knife into the seed. The knife should firmly lodge itself in the seed.

4 Gently turn the knife in a clockwise direction until the seed releases from the avocado half. Carefully pull the seed from the knife using a dish towel.

5 Gently slide a spoon between the avocado's flesh and the skin all the way around the half.

6 Lift the flesh out of the half with the spoon and prepare as needed.

7 Repeat steps 5 and 6 with the other avocado half.

Prepare Melons

Once you learn how easy it is to prepare melons, you'll find yourself buying them more frequently.

Melons come in all sizes and colors but there are basically three types—smooth-skinned muskmelons (like honeydew melons), net-skinned muskmelons (like cantaloupes) and watermelons.

Melons should be washed before peeling or cutting. Then, with muskmelons, you can cut them into wedges and serve with or without the peel. To prepare melons without the peel, slice off the top and bottom and cut off the rind (the melon's peel). After that, you simply cut the fruit in half, scoop out the seeds and cut up the halves. Watermelons can be peeled and cut in the same manner, but because the seeds are spread throughout the flesh it is not practical to remove them. However, you can buy seedless watermelon. Refrigerate ripe whole melons or store cut pieces of melon in sealed plastic bags in the fridge.

Interestingly, smooth-skinned winter squash can be prepared in the same way as melons.

Peel a Melon

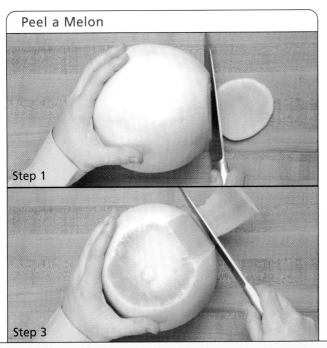

Step 1

Step 3

- In the photos, a honeydew is used to demonstrate how to peel a melon.

1 Place a melon on a cutting board and cut off both ends of the melon.

2 Turn the melon so that one of the cut ends is on the board.

3 Cut a slice of rind off the melon, starting at the top and cutting down, following the shape of the melon. After each slice, rotate the melon and make another cut until all of the rind has been removed.

Cut and Seed a Hollow Melon

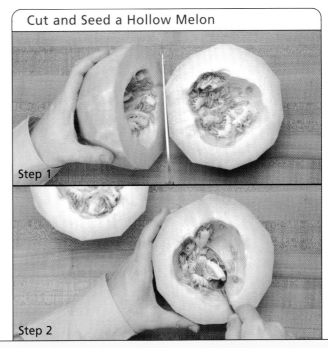

Step 1

Step 2

- The seeds of a hollow melon, such as a honeydew melon, are found in the melon's hollow center and are easy to remove.

1 Place the melon on a cutting board and cut it in half widthwise.

2 Using a spoon, scrape out the seeds from both halves of the melon and discard.

3 Turn each half cut side down and cut into wedges or as called for in the recipe.

Prepare Apples, Pears & Strawberries

When preparing such delectable treats as apple cake, poached pears or strawberry-rhubarb pie, you will need to know how to prepare apples, pears and strawberries. This typically involves peeling the fruit and removing its core.

Preparing apples and pears is time sensitive, since the fruit can brown if prepared too far in advance. To prevent this, brush the peeled and cut fruit with a bit of lemon juice or immerse it in acidulated water (8 cups of water mixed with the juice of one lemon) for no more than 2 hours.

While strawberries do not need to be peeled, you can remove the cores and stems in a process called hulling. Strawberry cores do not taste unpleasant, but they have a tough texture.

Before preparing apples, pears or strawberries, you should thoroughly wash the fruit.

Peel Apples & Pears

Core an Apple

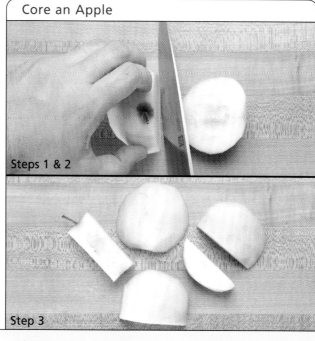

Steps 1 & 2

Step 3

- Peeling is the process of removing the skin from a fruit. In the photo, an apple is used to demonstrate peeling.

1 Holding the fruit in one hand, pull the blade of a vegetable peeler from the top of the fruit down to its base.

2 Rotate the fruit slightly and repeat step 2. Continue rotating and peeling until all of the skin has been removed.

- The core of an apple must be removed before using the apple in a recipe. This technique quickly and easily cuts the flesh away from the core.

1 Place the apple upright on a cutting board.

2 Using a chef's knife, cut one side from the apple, slicing close to the core.

3 Rotate the apple 1/4 turn and repeat step 2. Continue rotating and cutting until all 4 sides of the apple have been cut.

Tip *Are there any tools that will make hulling easier?*

You can simplify the process of hulling strawberries by purchasing a specialized tool called a tomato corer. As the name suggests, tomato corers were designed for use with tomatoes, but their serrated, disc-shaped metal heads are perfect for scooping the stems and cores out of strawberries.

Core a Pear

Step 1

Step 2

Hull a Strawberry

Stem

Core

- The core of a pear must be removed before using the pear in a recipe. This technique uses a melon baller to remove the core.

1 Place the pear on a cutting board and cut it in half lengthwise.

2 Holding one of the halves on the cutting board with one hand, use the other hand to scoop out the core with a melon baller.

3 Repeat step 2 with the other pear half.

- To prepare a strawberry for use in a recipe, the stem and small core may have to be removed in a process called hulling.

1 Using a paring knife, make a cone-shaped cut around the stem of the strawberry to remove the stem and small core.

- Never wash a hulled strawberry because it will absorb the water and become mushy.

Zest & Grate Citrus Fruit

You can add a little citrus zing to your recipes by using a couple of handy techniques that remove the flavorful peel from a citrus fruit.

Zesting removes thin strips of citrus peel, called zest, from the fruit. A tool called a citrus zester is commonly used for this task. A paring knife can also be used to zest, but you must be careful not to cut off any of the bitter, white layer on the underside of the peel, called the pith.

Citrus zest is commonly used as a garnish and in sauces. If a recipe calls for minced citrus zest, you can cut the zest into smaller pieces with a knife.

Grating involves removing tiny pieces of citrus peel. You can use a handheld grater with small holes to grate citrus fruit. Grated citrus peel is often used to add citrus flavors to foods like lemon pie filling and cakes.

Citrus fruits should be rinsed before you zest or grate them.

Zesting Citrus Fruit

Step 1

Zest

Step 2

Grating Citrus Peel

Grated lime

- Zesting is the process of removing thin strips of peel from a citrus fruit with a handheld tool called a citrus zester.

1 Holding the fruit in one hand, use your other hand to position the edge of the citrus zester at the top of the fruit.

2 Using firm and even pressure, move the citrus zester downward to the bottom of the fruit.

3 Rotate the fruit and repeat steps 1 and 2 until you have enough zest.

- Grating is the process of removing tiny pieces of peel from a citrus fruit with a grater.

1 Hold a handheld grater at a 45-degree angle over a cutting board with the grater's rough side facing up and its top edge resting on the board.

2 Rub the citrus fruit downward against the rough side of the grater.

- Grate off only the colorful skin of the fruit. The white layer on the underside of the peel is bitter.

3 Rotate the fruit and repeat step 2 until you have enough grated peel.

Juice Citrus Fruits

Whether you want to enjoy a glass of freshly-squeezed orange juice or you are preparing a recipe that calls for fresh lemon juice, you will need to know how to juice a citrus fruit.

Juicing is the process of extracting the juice from a citrus fruit. To juice a citrus fruit, you use a pointed tool called a citrus reamer, though you can also use a citrus press or juicer.

If you do not have any of these tools handy, you can squeeze the juice out manually with your hand. Whether you use a tool or squeeze the juice manually, be sure to wash the citrus fruit first. Before juicing, you should also roll the citrus fruit firmly against the counter with your hand to maximize the amount of juice you can extract.

Juice a Citrus Fruit

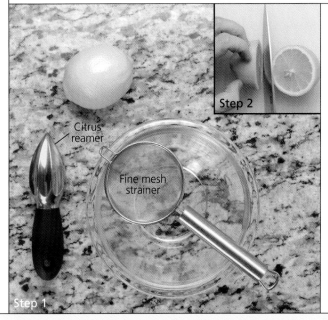

Citrus reamer

Fine mesh strainer

Step 1

Step 2

Step 3

Step 4

- Juicing often involves using a pointed tool, called a citrus reamer, to squeeze the juice out of halved citrus fruits. In the photos, a lemon is used to demonstrate juicing with a reamer.

1 Place a fine mesh strainer over a bowl.

- The strainer will separate any pulp and seeds from the juice that is squeezed out of the fruit.

2 Place the citrus fruit you wish to juice on a cutting board and cut it in half widthwise.

3 Holding one of the halves over the strainer and bowl, push the pointed end of the reamer into the center of the fruit.

4 Twist the reamer with one hand while squeezing the fruit half with the other hand until all of the juice has been released.

5 Repeat steps 3 and 4 with the other half of the citrus fruit.

Break & Separate Eggs

Breaking and separating eggs are essential techniques for the chef at home. If you use the right technique when breaking eggs, you can say goodbye to pieces of eggshell showing up in your favorite dishes.

While separating eggs may seem intimidating, it's not as difficult as it appears. If your recipe calls for separated egg yolks or whites, it's time to get cracking, but remember the following points. During shell-to-shell transfer, bacteria on the outside of the shell may come in contact with the egg white and yolk, so eggs separated in this manner must be fully cooked when served. Raw egg yolks covered with plastic wrap will last about three days in the fridge, and raw whites stored in the same manner will last about four days.

Break an Egg

Steps 1, 2 & 3

Step 4

1 Place a small bowl on the counter.

2 Pick up an egg in one hand.

3 Gently tap the middle of the egg against the counter, to create a crack in the shell.

- Take care when tapping an egg against the counter. If tapped too hard, the shell will shatter and leave the egg full of shell fragments.

4 Gently place your thumbs slightly inside the crack.

5 Slowly pull the two halves of the shell apart, allowing the egg to fall into the bowl.

- You should not break an egg directly into a bowl containing other ingredients. Shell fragments are easier to remove from a bowl that does not contain other ingredients.

- If a shell fragment falls into the bowl, you can use a knife tip to push the piece of eggshell to the side of the bowl where it can be easily removed.

Tip

How do I use an egg separator?

To use an egg separator to separate the white from the yolk, place the egg separator over a small bowl. Crack the egg open and let the yolk fall into the center of the separator. The egg white will slip through the slots in the egg separator and into the bowl. Place the separated yolk into a second bowl. If the separated whites are completely free of yolk, pour them into a third bowl before you separate the next egg.

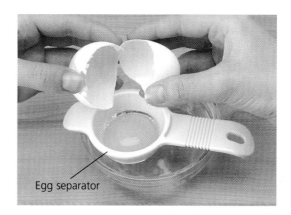

Egg separator

Separate an Egg

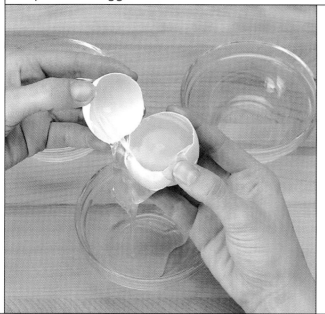

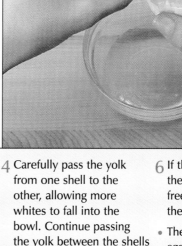

Yolks   Whites

1 Place three small bowls on the counter.

2 Gently tap an egg against the counter to create a crack in the shell.

3 Holding the egg upright over the first bowl, slowly pull off the top half of the eggshell. Be sure the yolk stays in the bottom half. Some of the whites will slip out and fall into the bowl.

4 Carefully pass the yolk from one shell to the other, allowing more whites to fall into the bowl. Continue passing the yolk between the shells until most of the whites are in the first bowl.

5 Pour the yolk into the second bowl.

6 If the separated whites in the first bowl are completely free of yolk, pour them into the third bowl.

• The yolk-free whites of each egg you separate should be poured into the third bowl before separating the next egg.

Beat & Fold in Egg Whites

Before preparing your mother's lemon meringue pie or your grandmother's angel food cake, you must know how to beat egg whites. To reduce your risk of salmonella poisoning, you may want to use pasteurized eggs if a recipe calls for egg whites that will not be cooked after.

Beating egg whites involves mixing the egg whites slowly at first and then rapidly beating them until the whites stiffen into peaks.

Your bowl and beaters must be completely clean and dry for whites to stiffen properly.

After beating egg whites, you can use a technique called folding to gently add the whites to another mixture without deflating them.

Beaten egg whites should be used immediately after preparation. They will begin to deflate as soon as you stop mixing.

Beat Egg Whites

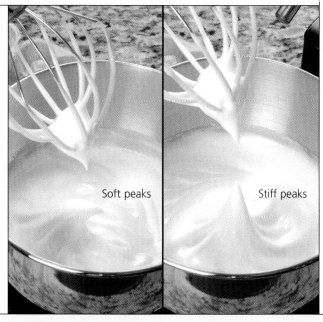

Soft peaks

Stiff peaks

- The reason for beating egg whites is to add tiny air bubbles that will increase the size and lighten the density of the whites.

1 Place the egg whites (free of any traces of yolk) in a large, clean bowl.

2 Using an electric mixer or flexible balloon whisk, begin beating the whites slowly.

3 When the whites become foamy, start beating them rapidly.

4 When the whites become thick and shiny, stop beating and lift the beaters or whisk. If the whites form smooth, pointed mounds that droop slightly, you have reached the "soft peaks" stage. If the recipe calls for "stiff peaks," continue beating the whites until they form smooth, pointed mounds that stand up straight.

- If you beat your whites too much, they will begin to dry out and you will have to start again with new egg whites. It is better to slightly under-beat your egg whites than to over-beat them.

Tip

What type of bowl should I use to beat egg whites?

You will achieve the best results with a copper bowl, but stainless steel, ceramic or glass bowls will also work well. You should never use a plastic or aluminum bowl.

Tip

When beating egg whites, why would I use cream of tartar?

Adding cream of tartar will help improve the stability and volume of your beaten egg whites. You can find cream of tartar in the baking section of your grocery store. You should never use cream of tartar when using a copper bowl. To use cream of tartar, add 1/8 teaspoon for each egg white in step 3 on page 94. White vinegar can be used as a substitute for cream of tartar.

Fold in Beaten Egg Whites

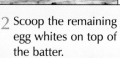

- Beaten egg whites are delicate, so you must use a technique called folding to combine them with another mixture.

1 Scoop 1/4 of the beaten egg whites into the mixture with which they are to be combined. Stir thoroughly to lighten the batter.

2 Scoop the remaining egg whites on top of the batter.

3 In a circular motion, cut along the inside of the bowl with a wide spatula, going down to the bottom of the bowl.

4 As you continue the circular motion, gently scoop some of the batter from the bottom of the bowl to the surface with the spatula.

5 Give the bowl a 1/4 turn and repeat steps 3 and 4.

6 Continue folding the mixture until only a few streaks of the whites are visible in the batter. Use the mixture immediately.

Cook & Peel Hard-Cooked Eggs

Hard-cooked eggs, also referred to as hard-boiled eggs, are a nutritional powerhouse and a great snack on the go. Making hard-cooked eggs is easy—if you can add eggs to a pot and boil water, you'll be able to hard-cook eggs in a snap. You will need to adjust the cooking time if you are using different sized eggs. If you are using jumbo eggs, allow them to sit

for 18 minutes in step 5 below. Medium eggs should sit for 12 minutes. Be sure to cool the eggs immediately after cooking or an unattractive green ring will surround the yolks, and always refrigerate the hard-cooked eggs in the shell, unless serving within the next few hours. Hard-cooked eggs should be eaten within a week.

Make Hard-Cooked Eggs

- Eggs referred to in this technique are large eggs.

1 Place the eggs in a saucepan, arranging them in a single layer.

- Stacking eggs in more than one layer may lead to uneven cooking and breakage.

2 Fill the saucepan with cold water until the water level is 1 inch above the eggs. Add 1 teaspoon of salt to the water.

3 Move the saucepan onto a stove burner and turn up the heat to bring the water to a boil.

4 After the water has been boiling for 30 seconds, place a lid on the saucepan, turn the heat off and move the saucepan to an unheated burner.

5 Allow the eggs to sit in the hot water for 15 minutes.

6 Place the saucepan in the sink and remove the lid. Using the tap, run a continuous stream of cold water into the saucepan for 2 minutes.

7 After 2 minutes, turn off the tap and allow the eggs to sit in the cold water for 3 minutes.

Tip

What does a fully cooked hard-cooked egg look like?

Because there's no way to tell if shell-on eggs are overdone or underdone, you must wait until the shell is removed to find out. This makes monitoring cooking time crucial. The yolk of a fully cooked egg is firm but velvety and is a uniform yellow, and the white is firm, but not rubbery. Underdone hard-cooked eggs will have a soft or runny yolk that is darker in the center. Overdone hard-cooked eggs will have a hard, crumbly yolk.

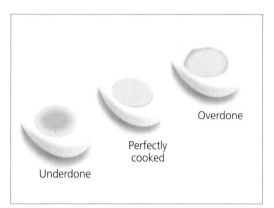

Overdone

Perfectly cooked

Underdone

Peel Hard-Cooked Eggs

Step 3

1 Once the hard-cooked eggs have cooled off, pick the eggs out of the saucepan and place on the counter. Pour the cold water out of the saucepan.

2 Place the eggs back in the saucepan and cover with the lid.

3 Holding the lid firmly with one hand, shake the saucepan over the sink for 10 seconds to crack the shells of the eggs inside.

4 Remove an egg from the saucepan.

5 Starting at the largest end of the egg, begin to peel off the shell.

• If you have difficulty removing the eggshell, try placing the egg under running cold water as you peel the egg. The shell should come off more easily.

6 Repeat steps 4 and 5 for each egg you want to peel.

Working With Fresh Herbs

If you think herbs are crunchy, dried up leaves that come in a jar, fresh herbs will be a welcome wake-up call for your taste buds. Fresh herbs give recipes flavorful dimensions that dried herbs cannot always match.

Today, fresh herbs can be found in the produce department of most grocery stores year-round. Some of the most popular varieties include thyme, parsley, cilantro, oregano, rosemary and basil. Fresh herbs are used in many recipes including butters, herbed mashed potatoes and homemade salad dressings. Just remember that fresh herbs can be milder than dried herbs, so you may need to add more fresh herbs when substituting for dried herbs.

Fresh herbs need a bit of preparation before being used. They must be washed and the leaves are usually removed from the stems. In the steps below, you will learn how to prepare various types of fresh herbs.

Preparing Herbs with Hard Stems

Steps 1 & 2

Step 3

Preparing Herbs with Soft Stems

Steps 1 & 2

Step 3

- The leaves of herbs with stiff, inedible stems, such as rosemary and thyme, are sometimes removed before the herbs are used.

1 Separate a stem from the bunch. Remove any branches from the stem so you have just a single stem.

2 Firmly grasp the top of the stem with one hand. Using your other hand, pinch the stem between your thumb and index finger just below where you are holding the stem.

3 Slide your pinched thumb and finger down the length of the stem. The leaves should easily come off.

- Herbs that have soft stems, such as dill and tarragon, can be simply chopped without having to separate the leaves from the stems.

1 Place the bunch of herbs on a cutting board.

2 Cut the approximate amount of herbs you need from the bunch.

3 Gather the herbs into a tight bundle, and make widthwise cuts across the herbs. Continue chopping the herbs until cut to the desired size.

4 If you need more herbs, repeat steps 1 to 3.

Tip

What is the best way to wash herbs?

Fresh herbs should be washed just before they are used. To wash herbs that are still on the stem, swish them around in a bowl of cold water so that any grit falls to the bottom of the water in the bowl. Parsley and cilantro leaves should be washed after being removed from their stems. Use a fine mesh strainer to hold the cut-off parsley or cilantro leaves in the bowl of water. All herbs should then be dried in a salad spinner or by gently blotting with paper towels.

Tip

How do I store fresh herbs?

Herbs can be wrapped in damp paper towels and stored in an open plastic bag in the fridge. Be sure that the bag remains open because the herbs need fresh air circulation. If you notice that the paper towels are drying out, replace them with new damp paper towels. Herbs will generally last in the fridge for about a week.

Shaving Herbs

Making Chiffonade Cuts

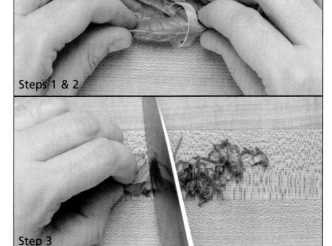

Steps 1 & 2

Step 3

- The leaves of bushy herbs, such as parsley and cilantro, can be easily shaved off their stems with a sharp chef's knife.

1 Grasp the whole bunch by the stems.

2 Holding the bunch over a paper towel, use a sharp chef's knife to shave the leaves off of the bunch in a smooth downward motion.

3 Turn the bunch and repeat step 2. Continue rotating and shaving until you have removed the amount of leaves you need from the bunch.

- The leaves of broad-leafed herbs, such as basil and sage, can be quickly and easily cut into fine strips using a technique called chiffonade.

1 Pick 5 or 6 individual leaves from their stems and stack them on a cutting board.

2 Roll the leaves lengthwise into a long, cigar-shaped bundle.

3 Cut very thin strips across the width of the bundle.

Stovetop Basics

If you are new to cooking, it's a good idea to become familiar with your stove. The first step is to read the instruction manual that came with your stove.

Below, we cover some basic guidelines for cooking on a stovetop and some safety tips.

Electric stove

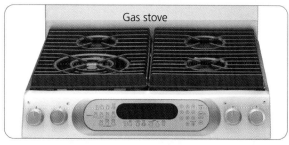
Gas stove

ELECTRIC & GAS STOVES

There are two types of stoves—electric and gas. Fortunately, cooking methods and times mentioned in recipes are the same whether you are using an electric or gas stove.

One thing to keep in mind, though, is that electric stovetops react slower to temperature changes than gas stovetops. For example, if you have a pot of water that is boiling over, you can simply reduce the heat on a gas stove to stop the water from boiling over. On an electric stove, you have to reduce the heat and remove the pot from the burner for a minute or so until the burner cools slightly.

HEAT LEVELS

Some stoves have dials with heat level indications on them, such as high, medium and low. Other stoves have dials that feature numbers from 1 to 10. Since most recipes give you a heat level for stovetop cooking, this chart provides a general guideline for what number setting corresponds to what heat level. You should refer to the instruction manual that came with your stove for more specific information.

HEAT LEVEL	DIAL SETTING
Low	1 – 2
Medium-Low	3 – 4
Medium	5 – 6
Medium-High	7 – 8
High	9 – 10

SAFETY TIPS

- Keep pan and pot handles pointed toward the center of the stovetop to prevent the handle from being bumped.

- Never leave a pan or pot of oil unattended on the stove when the burner is turned on.

- Use the burner size that best fits the pot or pan you are cooking in.

- Use oven mitts when handling pots and pans. The handles of some pots and pans can get hot enough to burn you.

- Beware of escaping steam when lifting the lids off pots and pans.

Simmering

Simmering is a cooking technique in which you cook liquids at a temperature just below the boiling point. You will know that a liquid is simmering when tiny bubbles rise slowly and break gently at the liquid's surface. You can simmer liquids on their own or cook other foods in the simmering liquid.

Dishes that are commonly simmered include soups, stews and sauces. Recipes often call for both boiling and simmering, instructing you to bring a liquid to a full boil and then reduce the heat and allow the liquid to simmer for a period of time.

Liquids can be simmered covered or uncovered, depending on the recipe. Keep in mind that you may have to adjust the heat level under the pot or pan in order to keep the liquid at a simmer.

Simmering

Step 3

Step 4

- Simmering is a cooking technique in which you cook liquids at a temperature just below the boiling point. Foods that are commonly simmered include soups, stews and sauces.

1 To simmer food, add a liquid, such as broth, to a pot on the stove.

2 Heat the liquid until it boils, with large bubbles rapidly breaking the surface of the liquid.

3 Carefully add any food you want to simmer to the pot. The liquid may stop boiling when you add the food.

4 Allow the liquid to return to a boil. Then reduce the heat to bring the contents to a simmer, with tiny bubbles rising slowly and gently breaking at the liquid's surface.

- Some recipes require you to simmer foods for a long period of time. You may need to adjust the heat level occasionally to ensure that the liquid remains at a simmer for the entire cooking time.

Poaching

Poaching is a method of gently cooking food in liquid that is heated to just under the boiling point. When you poach food, you preserve the food's texture while infusing it with the flavor of the poaching liquid.

Poaching is ideal for cooking whole or firm fish, such as salmon, catfish and tuna. When poaching several pieces of fish, make sure the pan isn't overcrowded. Arrange the pieces in a single layer and leave room for the liquid to circulate between the pieces. Fish is cooked when the flesh flakes apart with a fork.

Poached eggs are great for brunch or as an appetizer. Vinegar is added to the poaching liquid to help keep the egg white together. A poached egg is cooked when the white has solidified around the yolk, which should be thickened but soft.

Poaching Fish

- Depending on the recipe, fish can be poached in water or a flavored poaching liquid, such as vegetable stock.

1 Add the poaching liquid to a large, high-sided sauté pan. Place the pan on a burner and turn up the heat to bring the liquid to a boil.

2 When the liquid boils, turn down the heat so the liquid is at a low simmer (barely bubbling).

3 Gently lower the fish into the liquid. The fish should be totally immersed.

4 Allow the fish to cook, checking it frequently for doneness. As the fish cooks, you may need to adjust the heat so the poaching liquid remains at a low simmer.

5 When the fish is done, gently remove it from the pan using a large perforated skimmer.

What other foods can I poach?

Besides fish and eggs, you can poach foods such as poultry, vegetables, fruit and other types of seafood, such as lobster and shrimp. You can also vary the poaching liquid by using stock for poultry and a light sugar syrup or wine for fruit. Keep in mind that the fruit you use for poaching should be firm but ripe.

 How should I serve my poached eggs?

Eggs Florentine is a popular dish which consists of a toasted English muffin topped with sautéed spinach, a poached egg and Hollandaise sauce. For a healthy, well-balanced alternative to Eggs Florentine, try serving your poached eggs on top of our Summery Spinach Salad (see page 138). Just omit the pine nuts and orange segments in the salad and serve with a toasted whole-wheat English muffin on the side.

Poaching Eggs

Step 3

Step 2

Step 4

Step 6

- Poached eggs are cooked in salted water and vinegar.

1 Add 2 to 3 inches of water to a large sauté pan. Add 1 teaspoon of salt and 1 tablespoon of vinegar.

2 Place the pan on a burner and turn up the heat to bring the water to a boil. When the water boils, turn down the heat so the water is at a low simmer (barely bubbling).

3 Break an egg into a small bowl, being careful not to break the yolk.

4 Holding the bowl close to the surface of the water, slowly tip the egg into the water.

5 Cook for 2 1/2 to 4 minutes, depending on how firm you would like the yolk.

6 When the egg has cooked, lift the egg out of the water with a large perforated skimmer, being careful not to break the yolk.

7 Gently pat the egg dry with a paper towel before serving.

Boiling, Parboiling & Blanching

Few things are simpler than boiling water, but it is crucial for three important cooking methods—boiling, parboiling and blanching.

Boiling involves completely cooking food in boiling water. Parboiling is similar, only the food is removed from the boiling water just before it is completely cooked. This brings out the color in vegetables and softens them so they can be finished using another cooking method, such as sautéing. Blanching involves barely cooking food in boiling water for as little as a few seconds to less than two minutes. This can be used to loosen skin from fruits and vegetables.

When boiling, parboiling or blanching vegetables, a tablespoon of salt in the water will add flavor and bring out the color of your vegetables.

Ice water is sometimes used to preserve the color and texture of foods just after they have been boiled, parboiled or blanched. This cold water is called an ice bath and the process is referred to as shocking.

Boiling, Parboiling & Blanching

- Boiling, parboiling and blanching are three ways of fully or partially cooking foods using boiling water.

1 Place the lid on a large saucepan or stockpot half-filled with cold water. Bring the water to a rapid boil, with large bubbles quickly rising to the surface.

2 Remove the lid. If you are cooking vegetables, add a tablespoon of salt to the boiling water.

3 Using a large perforated skimmer, carefully lower the food into the boiling water.

4 When boiling, leave the food in the boiling water until the food is fully cooked.

Note: For boiling times for vegetables, see page 108.

- When parboiling, leave the food in the boiling water until the food is almost cooked.

- When blanching, leave the food in the boiling water for 15 seconds to 2 minutes, depending on the food and the recipe.

5 Using a large perforated skimmer, remove the food from the boiling water.

How can I save time when preparing cooked vegetables?

Parboiling followed by an ice bath is a great way to prepare vegetables ahead of time. Simply parboil your vegetables and give them an ice bath. After draining, you can refrigerate the vegetables for up to a day. Then all you have to do is sauté them for a couple of minutes in oil and add flavorings such as salt, pepper, garlic and herbs just prior to serving.

How can I use blanched vegetables?

Blanched vegetables are a better-tasting substitute for some raw vegetables. The next time you serve vegetables with dip, take the time to quickly blanch and shock the broccoli and cauliflower. This process will remove the harsher flavors and dry hard texture that these raw vegetables possess. It will also help bring out the vivid color of the broccoli.

Ice Bath

- After boiling, parboiling or blanching food, you can place the food in an ice bath to immediately stop the cooking process.

1 Fill a large bowl two-thirds full with cold water and ice cubes.

2 Perform steps 1 to 4 on page 104 to boil, parboil or blanch the food.

3 Using a large perforated skimmer, remove the food from the boiling water and place it in the bowl of ice water for 1 to 2 minutes.

4 Once the food is chilled, use a large perforated skimmer to remove it from the ice water. Place the food into a colander, removing any pieces of ice.

5 After the food has drained completely, remove the food from the colander and pat dry the food with a paper towel, if needed.

- If you plan to sauté the food in oil or freeze the food, you must completely dry the food.

Steaming

Steaming is a very gentle cooking method which involves cooking food over steam created by boiling water in a covered pan. As one of the best ways to keep a food's shape, color and nutrients intact, steaming is often used to cook delicate vegetables and seafood.

A common way to steam food is by using a collapsible steamer basket which fits into a saucepan. There are other types of steamers, such as a saucepan with a steamer insert or a bamboo steamer with a fitted lid. See page 21 for more information on steaming utensils.

Whichever steaming utensil you choose, be sure the food does not touch the boiling water. This will cause part of the food to be boiled rather than steamed. It's also important to monitor the water level as you steam. You may need to add more water to ensure that the pot does not boil dry.

Steaming

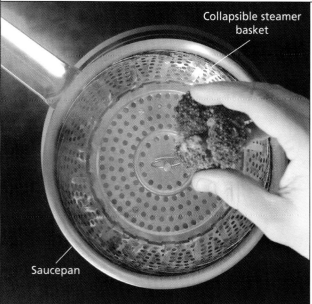

Collapsible steamer basket

Saucepan

1 Place a medium saucepan containing water and a collapsible steamer basket over medium-high heat. The water level should be just below the bottom of the steamer basket.

2 Allow the water in the saucepan to come to a gentle boil, with steam rising from the surface.

3 Using your fingers, carefully place the food you want to steam, such as broccoli, in the steamer basket.

4 Cover the saucepan and allow the food to steam until it reaches the desired degree of doneness. For information on vegetable steaming times, see page 108.

5 Using oven mitts, carefully lift the steamer basket out of the saucepan and place it on a heatproof surface.

6 Using tongs, remove the food from the steamer insert.

- You can now serve the food or place the food in an ice bath (see page 105) to stop the cooking process.

Sweating Vegetables

Having to sweat in the kitchen a little bit, isn't always a bad thing. Sweating is actually a culinary term for the process of gently cooking vegetables in a small amount of oil or butter just long enough for the vegetables to soften but not long enough that they turn brown.

You may notice that some recipes will instruct you to cook some cut-up onion in oil that is not too hot. This is an example of sweating and causes the onion to soften, lose some of its pungency and begin to sweeten. No browning of the onion should take place.

Many times in French cooking, cut carrots and celery are gently cooked along with onions to soften and bring out the sweetness of all three vegetables. The classic combination of onions, carrots and celery is called mirepoix.

Sweating Vegetables

Translucent onions

- Sweating involves cooking cut-up vegetables in a small amount of oil and/or butter that is not too hot.

1 Place a skillet over medium heat.

2 Add 2 tablespoons of extra virgin olive oil to the skillet.

3 Add the vegetables, such as a chopped onion, to the skillet.

4 Allow the vegetables to cook, stirring occasionally using a wooden spoon.

5 The sweating is complete when the vegetables are slightly softened but not browned.

- When sweating onions, the onions will be translucent when they are done.

Cooking Vegetables

Most vegetables can be cooked using several different methods. This chart outlines how you can cook a variety of vegetables three different ways—boiling, steaming and roasting.

Boiling cooks vegetables by completely immersing them in boiling or simmering (barely bubbling) water in an uncovered pot. This method is easy, but it can cause the vegetables to lose some of their nutrients.

Steaming cooks vegetables over the steam created by boiling water in a covered container. This method helps vegetables retain their color, texture and nutrients.

Roasting cooks vegetables in the heat of an oven. This method concentrates and sweetens the flavors of many vegetables. Prior to roasting, toss the vegetables with some extra virgin olive oil and a sprinkling of salt, pepper and other seasonings to suit your tastes. Unless directed otherwise, roast the vegetables uncovered on a baking sheet that has been lined with parchment paper or lightly oiled.

Each method below lists a range of cooking times since smaller pieces cook faster than larger pieces. The actual time will depend on the size of your vegetables, so check for doneness at the earliest time and continue to check until they are done. To check for doneness, you can pierce vegetables with a paring knife.

"Crisp-tender" is the point at which vegetables are still slightly firm but can be pierced with a paring knife.

VEGETABLE	PREP. NOTES	BOIL (Uncovered)	STEAM (Covered)	ROAST (425°F)	DONENESS
Asparagus	Whole, with bottom end of asparagus snapped off	5 to 8 minutes, in a skillet half filled with simmering salted water	7 to 10 minutes	5 to 10 minutes	Done when slightly droopy, not limp
Beans, Green String and Yellow Wax	Whole, with ends trimmed	4 to 8 minutes	4 to 8 minutes	Not recommended	Done when barely tender, not soft
Broccoli	Cut into florets or clusters, stalks peeled and sliced	5 to 6 minutes	5 to 7 minutes	Not recommended	Done when stalks are tender but still firm, should be vivid green
Brussels Sprouts	Whole or halved; cut an "X" at the bottom of whole sprouts	8 to 15 minutes	8 to 15 minutes	20 to 30 minutes, in oven-safe dish with 3 tbsp of water, until lightly browned	Done when tender, not mushy

VEGETABLE	PREP. NOTES	BOIL (Uncovered)	STEAM (Covered)	ROAST (425°F)	DONENESS
Cabbage	Cut into wedges or quarters, loose and discolored leaves removed	7 to 20 minutes	7 to 20 minutes	Not recommended	Done when tender, not mushy
Carrots/Parsnips	Whole or cut into 1-inch chunks	6 to 8 minutes for pieces; 15 to 20 minutes for whole	6 to 8 minutes for pieces; 15 to 20 minutes for whole	35 to 45 minutes for pieces; 40 to 60 minutes for whole	Done when barely tender, not soft
Cauliflower	Cut into florets or clusters	5 to 6 minutes	5 to 7 minutes	30 to 40 minutes (until lightly browned)	Done when stem end of florets are tender but still firm
Leeks	Halved lengthwise; dark green tops and root ends removed	10 to 20 minutes, in a skillet half filled with salted water	10 to 20 minutes	10 to 20 minutes in oven-safe dish with 3 tbsp of water	Done when very tender, will be chewy if undercooked
Peas in Shell	Strings on snow peas removed	2 to 4 minutes	2 to 4 minutes	Not recommended	Done when crisp-tender, not soft or mushy
Peas without Shell	Peas removed from shell	2 to 4 minutes	2 to 4 minutes	Not recommended	Done when crisp-tender, not soft or mushy
Potatoes	Peeled or unpeeled; large potatoes cut into 1-inch chunks	Place in cold water, bring to boil. Add salt and boil for 15 to 30 minutes	20 to 25 minutes	40 to 60 minutes	Done when tender
Summer Squash	Whole, halved or sliced into 1-inch chunks	2 to 5 minutes	4 to 6 minutes	Not recommended	Done when crisp-tender
Sweet Potatoes	Whole or cut into 1-inch chunks	Place in cold water, bring to boil. Add salt and boil for 15 to 30 minutes	20 to 40 minutes	30 to 50 minutes	Done when tender
Winter Squash and Pumpkin	Cut in half or into wedges; or peeled and cut into 1-inch chunks	15 to 25 minutes (peeled squash/pumpkin only)	20 to 40 minutes (peeled squash/pumpkin only)	30 to 60 minutes	Done when very tender

Cooking Pasta

Great pasta dishes start with perfectly cooked pasta. Pasta is cooked perfectly when it is cooked to *al dente* (pronounced "al dentay"), which means the pasta is still firm, but is tender enough not to stick to your teeth.

When cooking pasta, start with a pot filled with lots of cold water to help ensure that the pasta pieces will not stick together as they cook. Once the water is boiling, you can add salt to the water to enhance the flavor of the pasta. Depending on the type of pasta, fresh pasta can take about 30 seconds to 3 minutes to cook, while dried pasta usually cooks in 5 to 10 minutes.

Rinsing cooked pasta in cold water is required for dishes such as pasta salad, but if you intend to serve your pasta with sauce, do not rinse the pasta or the sauce will not stick to it.

Cooking Pasta

1 Fill a stockpot two-thirds full with cold water and then place the lid on the stockpot.

2 Bring the water to a rapid boil, with large bubbles quickly rising to the surface.

3 Remove the lid and add a tablespoon of salt to the boiling water to flavor the water.

Note: Do not add oil to the water. Oil will prevent the sauce from properly coating the pasta.

4 Place a colander in your sink to drain the pasta when it is cooked.

5 Read the package directions to determine how long to cook the pasta. You want to cook the pasta to the shortest time indicated.

6 Add the pasta to the rapidly boiling water and then immediately stir the pasta to keep it from sticking together. Continue to stir the pasta until the water returns to a rapid boil.

7 As the pasta cooks, keep the water at a rapid boil and occasionally stir the pasta.

Note: You may need to reduce the heat slightly to prevent the water from boiling over.

Tip

Is there another way to cook pasta for serving with a sauce?

When the pasta is about one minute away from *al dente* and the sauce is simmering in a large sauté pan, turn off the burner under the pasta pot. Remove about 1/2 cup of the pasta water and set it aside. Drain the pasta in a colander, without shaking, and then add the pasta to the sauté pan, increasing the heat to medium high. Toss the pasta with the sauce to completely coat the pasta. If the mixture seems too dry, add up to 1/4 cup of the pasta water until it reaches the desired consistency. This process should take about one minute.

8 As the end of the cooking time approaches, remove a piece of pasta from the stockpot.

9 Allow the pasta to cool for a moment and then bite into the pasta.

• The pasta is cooked to *al dente* when it is firm, but no longer crunchy.

• If the pasta sticks to your teeth or has a white-colored, raw looking center, the pasta is not quite cooked. If the pasta is soft, it is overcooked.

10 When the pasta is cooked to *al dente*, immediately drain the pasta into the colander in your sink.

11 Shake the colander to help drain the pasta.

• If you are going to use the pasta in a salad or baked dish, rinse the pasta under cold running water to stop the cooking process and prevent the pasta from sticking together.

12 To serve the pasta with sauce, immediately place the pasta in a serving bowl or on plates and add the sauce to the pasta.

Deep Frying & Shallow Frying

Deep frying and shallow frying are two common methods of frying food in oil.

Deep frying cooks food by completely immersing it in hot oil. This works well with shrimp, chicken, French fries and doughnuts. Deep frying requires caution because of the high temperature of the oil. Never leave hot oil unattended.

Shallow frying cooks food in a skillet where the food is only partially immersed in oil.

Shallow frying works well with breaded fish and small foods like spring rolls and egg rolls.

For either method, it is best to use safflower or canola oil. These oils have a relatively high smoking point, meaning they do not start to smoke until they reach higher temperatures.

Fry food in small batches and, after each batch, skim off any bits of food that remain in the oil. Otherwise, the bits will burn and affect the flavor of subsequent batches.

Deep Frying

Step 4

Step 5

- When you deep fry, you cook food in hot oil that is deep enough to completely cover the food.

1 If desired, bread the food you want to deep fry (see page 75).

2 Place a large saucepan half-filled with safflower or canola oil over medium-high heat.

3 Allow the oil to get very hot, so the surface of the oil is shimmering and rippling slightly, but not boiling.

4 Using your fingers, carefully lower each piece of food into the hot oil. Be careful not to touch the oil or crowd the pieces in the oil.

5 When the food is cooked, remove the pieces using a large perforated skimmer or slotted spoon.

6 Place the cooked pieces on a baking sheet, cooling rack or large plate lined with a double layer of paper towels to drain.

7 If desired, add salt or other seasonings, to taste, while the food is still hot.

Tip

Why do some deep-fried foods have a crunchy crust?

Deep-fried foods that have a crust have often been coated in a thick liquid batter prior to being deep fried. Tempura is a popular type of batter used on vegetables and shrimp. With battered foods, you dip the foods into a batter mixture by hand and then carefully lower the food into the oil. To avoid splattering, you should dip the bottom of the battered food into the oil before releasing it.

Tip

What is the best method for making French fries?

The best way to make French fries is to precook them by deep frying them in hot oil until the fries begin to turn just slightly golden. At that point, remove and drain the fries. Then, just prior to serving, deep fry them again in very hot oil until they reach the desired degree of doneness. This method gives the fries great texture and crispness.

Shallow Frying

- Shallow frying works well for breaded foods. For information on breading, see page 75.

1 Place a skillet over medium-high heat.

2 When the skillet is hot, carefully add enough safflower or canola oil so the oil will come half-way up the sides of the food you want to fry.

3 When the oil is hot, use your fingers to carefully place pieces of food, such as breaded chicken cutlets, in the oil, leaving space all around each piece.

4 Allow the food to fry until it is browned on the bottom. Using tongs, turn the food and allow it to fry on the other side until it is browned and cooked through.

5 Using tongs, remove the cooked pieces and place them on a baking sheet, cooling rack or large plate lined with a double layer of paper towels to drain.

6 If desired, add salt or other seasonings, to taste, while the food is still hot.

Sautéing, Pan Frying & Stir-Frying

Sautéing, pan frying and stir-frying are similar ways of cooking foods at higher temperatures with oil.

Sautéing uses oil to quickly cook smaller pieces of food at higher temperatures in a skillet or sauté pan. Food that is being sautéd should be constantly moved around the pan, either with a utensil or by shaking the pan to prevent burning. Pan frying is similar to sautéing, but it usually involves larger pieces of food which do not get moved around

frequently. For example, you would sauté mushrooms but pan fry a boneless chicken breast.

Stir-frying is an Asian cooking method that is similar to sautéing. Traditionally, stir-frying means to cook small pieces of food in extremely hot oil for a very short time. In North American kitchens, however, the terms sauté and stir-fry are basically interchangeable.

When sautéing, pan frying or stir-frying, use extra virgin olive oil, canola or safflower oil.

Sautéing, Pan Frying & Stir-Frying

- Sautéing, pan frying and stir-frying all involve cooking food in oil at higher heat.

1 Place a large sauté pan or wok over medium-high heat and allow the pan to get very hot.

2 Carefully add 2 tablespoons of extra virgin olive oil, safflower or canola oil to the pan and allow it to heat up for about 20 seconds.

3 Carefully place the food you want to fry in the pan.

4 Allow the food to cook, constantly tossing and moving the food with wooden spoons.

5 When the food is cooked to the desired level of doneness, remove the food from the pan.

Reducing

They say that less is more. In the case of reducing, this is certainly true. Reducing is the process of rapidly boiling a liquid so that it decreases in volume and becomes thicker and more flavorful. This is normally done in a saucepan and is often used to make sauces. If you have to reduce a liquid by half, it should be boiled until only half of the original volume remains.

Since reducing intensifies flavors, be sure to use liquids that contain little or no salt. Sauces made by reduction should be seasoned with salt and other flavorings only after they have been reduced. In addition to flavorings, butter and cream are sometimes added to reduced sauces to make them richer and glossier.

As you are reducing a liquid, it is best to stir as little as possible. Stirring brings down the temperature of the liquid and causes the reducing to take longer.

Reducing

- Reducing involves thickening a liquid to intensify its flavor. In this example, port wine is reduced to create a sauce that can be served over steak.

1 Place the liquid you want to reduce in a small saucepan. In this example, 2 cups of port wine and 1 tablespoon of red wine vinegar are used.

2 Place the saucepan over medium heat and bring the liquid to a boil, with large bubbles rapidly breaking the surface. Do not stir the liquid.

3 Allow the liquid to continue boiling until the amount called for in the recipe remains.

Note: In this example, we boil the liquid until 1/3 cup remains.

4 When the liquid has reduced to the desired amount, remove the sauce from the heat.

- To enhance the sauce, you can whisk in one tablespoon of butter. You can also add seasonings, such as salt and pepper, to taste.

Searing

Searing is the process of cooking a food's surface with extremely high heat. Usually performed on the stovetop in a skillet, sauté pan or Dutch oven, searing creates a tasty crust on food. After searing, food is often cooked using another method, such as stewing or braising.

Aside from creating the flavorful crust, searing meat also helps to seal in some of the meat's natural juices.

Meat and poultry are the food items that are seared most often. In fact, certain tender cuts of meat and thinner portions of boneless poultry can be seared until completely cooked.

Searing can cause a lot of smoke, so turn on your vent fan before starting. If you are searing more than one piece of meat at a time, make sure you leave space around each piece. If you don't, the temperature of the skillet will go down to the point where the meat will start to steam and begin to release its natural juices.

Searing

- Searing uses high temperatures to create a browned crust on all the surfaces of a piece of meat or poultry and seal in the natural juices of the food.

1 Place a skillet over medium-high heat and allow the skillet to get very hot.

2 Add a small amount of oil to the hot skillet or rub oil on all sides of the meat you want to sear.

3 Carefully place the food you want to sear in the pan, leaving space all around each piece.

4 Allow the food to sear in the pan until the bottom of the food has a deep brown crust. Then, using tongs, turn the food and allow it to sear on another side.

5 Repeat step 4 until all the surfaces of the food are seared.

- After the food is seared on all sides, you can continue cooking the food using a method such as stewing or braising (see page 118).

Deglazing

Deglazing dissolves those flavorful browned bits that are left in a pan after cooking into a delicious mixture. Cleaning your dishes has never tasted so good.

After cooking meat, poultry, fish or even vegetables, in a pan at higher temperatures and also after roasting, scrumptious browned bits often remain in the pan. Those browned bits are packed with flavor that shouldn't be wasted—enter deglazing. After the food and fat have been removed from the pan, simply add a liquid, such as wine, beer, stock or water, to the pan. Then turn up the heat and scrape the browned bits off the bottom of the pan. This technique turns those bits into a flavorful mixture that can be made into a delicious sauce or gravy.

Deglazing

- Deglazing means dissolving the flavor-packed browned bits that are stuck to a pan after food has been seared.

1 Sear your food (see page 116). Remove the seared food from the pan and place the food on a plate or in a bowl.

- If necessary, use a spoon to remove any fat from the pan.

2 Lower the heat under the pan to medium low and carefully add 1 to 2 cups of liquid, such as broth, beer or water.

3 Increase the heat to medium high and bring the liquid to a boil.

4 Using a wooden spoon, scrape the browned bits off the bottom of the pan and mix them with the liquid.

- Once the browned bits are lifted off the bottom of the pan, remove the pan from the burner so the mixture does not burn.

- You can now use the mixture as the flavor base for a sauce or gravy.

Stewing & Braising

If you love food that melts in your mouth, you must try stewing and braising. These cooking methods use moist heat to cook foods like meat, poultry, fish and vegetables.

With both stewing and braising, ingredients are often seared to give the food extra color and flavor. The food is then slowly cooked in liquid, such as wine or broth, and seasonings that eventually become a sauce.

Stewing is usually used to cook chunks of meat, fish, poultry or vegetables. Braising is more often used to cook larger cuts of meat. The amount of liquid used also sets the methods apart—stewed foods are completely covered in liquid, while braised foods are only partially covered in liquid.

Stewing & Braising

- Stewing and braising are methods of slow cooking in liquid. Stewing usually involves small chunks of food, while braising is better for large cuts of meat.

- In this example, we show stewing.

1 Before stewing or braising meat, poultry, fish or vegetables, you should sear the food you plan to cook to create a browned surface and seal in the food's juices. For information on searing, see page 116.

2 To stew or braise food, place the seared food and any other required ingredients and seasonings for the recipe in a Dutch oven.

3 Add a liquid, such as beer, water, juice or broth, to the Dutch oven.

What cuts of meat are best suited to stewing and braising?

Consider using bone-in cuts of meat such as beef short-ribs or bone-in blade roasts when stewing or braising. The bones in meats and poultry contribute a lot of flavor to any dish in which they are used. Bones also contain gelatin which helps to naturally thicken the sauce that is created when you stew or braise.

 Can I stew and braise completely on the stovetop?

Instead of finishing a stew or braise in the oven, you can stew or braise from start to finish on the stovetop. If you choose to stew or braise on the stovetop, be careful that the ingredients at the bottom of the pot don't scorch during the long cooking process. To prevent this, stir the pot occasionally and keep the temperature at a low simmer, allowing the mixture to gently bubble.

- When stewing food, the liquid should just cover the food in the Dutch oven.

- When braising food, the liquid should come about halfway up the food.

4 Place the Dutch oven on a burner over medium-high heat and allow the liquid to come to a boil, with large bubbles quickly rising to the surface.

5 Place a lid on the Dutch oven and place in a preheated oven, as directed in the recipe. The stew or braise will simmer in the oven.

6 Cook in the oven until the meat and vegetables are tender when pierced with a fork, or as directed in the recipe.

Roasting

Roasting is a method in which food is cooked uncovered in the oven, usually without the addition of any liquid.

Roasting creates concentrated flavors and appealing textures in food. It also helps to retain the juices of many foods. Ideally, roasted food has a browned, deliciously crusty exterior and a flavorful, juicy interior.

Roasting is a simple method that can be used for cooking roasts, chicken, turkey and fish.

Root vegetables, like onions, potatoes and carrots, are also excellent candidates for roasting as their natural sugars come out and their surfaces turn a golden brown when roasted.

After meat has been roasted, it needs to rest on a cutting board before being sliced for roughly 15 minutes for meat and 10 minutes for poultry. This resting period allows the juices to redistribute throughout the meat and prevents the loss of precious juices and accompanying dryness.

Roasting

- You can roast meat or poultry in an oven to obtain a juicy interior and a browned exterior.

1 Preheat the oven to the required temperature for the food you will roast.

2 Place the food you want to roast in a roasting pan and then place the pan in the preheated oven.

- When roasting poultry, you normally place it breast-side up in a roasting pan.

- During roasting, you can use a meat thermometer to check the internal temperature of the meat you are roasting.

3 To check the internal temperature, insert the meat thermometer into the center of the thickest part of the food, making sure you do not touch or go too near the bone, if the meat has bones.

What is basting?

Basting is the process of occasionally drizzling pan juices or another liquid over the top of food as it roasts. Generally, only poultry is basted. This helps to brown the exterior more evenly, stay moist and develop flavor. Contrary to what some people think, basting poultry results in a skin that is less crispy than if left untouched. So if you want a crisp skin on your roast chicken or turkey, don't baste it.

Why should I take meat out of the oven just before it reaches the desired temperature?

Believe it or not, roasted meat, poultry and fish continue to cook after they have been removed from the oven. The temperature at the center of the meat will increase anywhere from 5 to 20 percent, depending on the thickness of the meat and its level of doneness. In order to avoid overcooking, you should remove the meat just before it reaches the desired temperature.

Table of Temperatures for Roasting

FOOD	FINAL INTERNAL TEMPERATURE
Pork	160°F
Poultry	180°F
Beef, Lamb and Veal—Rare	140°F
Beef, Lamb and Veal—Medium-Rare	150°F
Beef, Lamb and Veal—Medium-Well	160°F
Beef, Lamb and Veal—Well Done	170°F

4 When the food is about 5 degrees less than the final desired internal temperature, remove the food from the oven.

5 Using tongs, carefully place the food on a cutting board, uncovered, to rest.

• Resting allows the juices to be evenly redistributed within the food. A whole chicken should rest for 10 minutes, while a whole turkey or a large piece of meat, such as a roast, should rest for 15 minutes before carving. Smaller portions of poultry or meat need to rest from 3 to 10 minutes, depending on size.

• When roasting food, you should use the instructions in the recipe you are following to determine the appropriate final internal temperature for the food.

• The chart above provides general guidelines for the final internal temperatures for roasted pork, poultry, beef, lamb and veal.

Baking Tips

Baking means to cook food in an oven using dry heat. Part art and part science, baking involves combining ingredients in the right proportions, using the proper equipment and cooking at a specific, consistent oven temperature. You should avoid performing any other activities while measuring or mixing ingredients for baking, since distractions can often lead to mistakes.

While you can bake almost any food, baked goods commonly refer to items such as cookies, cakes and loaves.

INGREDIENTS

The first step in successful baking is to read the recipe carefully and gather the ingredients before you start. Make sure you are using the freshest and highest-quality ingredients you can afford. To help ensure ingredients such as baking powder, baking soda and yeast are fresh, you should mark the date that you open each container. Once opened, keep these ingredients for only 6 months.

When gathering ingredients, make sure you take the time to prepare the ingredients as instructed in the recipe. For example, if a recipe calls for softened butter, you should wait for chilled butter to warm to room temperature. Never heat your butter to soften it unless instructed otherwise. If a recipe calls for room-temperature eggs, remove the eggs from the refrigerator 20 to 30 minutes before using them.

BAKING TOOLS AND PANS

Before you begin mixing ingredients, assemble all the baking tools you will need to prepare your recipe, such as pans, whisks, spatulas, pastry brushes and bowls.

When selecting the pans you will need, make sure you use the type and size of pan specified in the recipe. You should also take care to prepare the pan as instructed. For example, a recipe may ask you to line your pan with parchment paper or grease the pan. When greasing a pan, use a pastry brush to lightly but thoroughly brush on vegetable shortening or melted butter. If your recipe asks you to dust the greased pan with flour, sprinkle a small quantity of flour over the entire surface of the pan and then turn it upside down over the sink to tap out the excess flour.

MEASURE CAREFULLY

Accurately measuring ingredients is critical when baking. While improvisation and guesswork may work in other methods of cooking, it can have disastrous consequences in baking. Make sure you are using the right tools for measuring ingredients. Use liquid measuring cups for wet ingredients like milk and water, and dry measuring cups for dry and semi-solid ingredients such as flour and peanut butter.

MIX CAREFULLY

A recipe will specify the mixing times and techniques you must follow in order for baked goods to turn out properly. You can use a kitchen timer to keep track of mixing times so you do not over- or under-mix ingredients.

Some ingredients, such as baking soda, will be activated as soon as they are mixed, so try to move through the steps in a recipe as quickly as possible. Delays during preparation can prevent a recipe from turning out properly.

OVEN TEMPERATURES

To prepare for baking, allow the oven to preheat to the specified temperature for 20 minutes before baking.

Filling the oven with many pans will prevent air from circulating properly around the pans and prevent your food from baking evenly. Check the guidelines in your oven's manual before baking with multiple pans at once.

You should avoid opening the oven door during baking, as this will allow heat to escape and will cause the oven temperature to vary. You should only open the oven door to check for doneness.

COOL BAKED GOODS

Baked goods must be cooled before serving. Some baked goods, such as brownies, are served out of the pan and can be cooled in the pan on a cooling rack. For cakes and loaves that must be removed from the pan, place the pan on a cooling rack and let it stand for 10 to 15 minutes. You can then run a knife along the inside of the pan to release the item from the sides of the pan and invert it onto a large plate. Then use the plate to flip the item onto the cooling rack right side up.

Recipes

Every home chef needs a collection of recipes that taste great and are sure to impress. This section will provide you with a wide variety of delicious dishes that are easy to prepare. You will find everything from starters and side dishes to main courses and baked goods. Several vegetarian options are included as well.

Cheesy Bean Quesadillas

These Cheesy Bean Quesadillas are terrific, whether you serve them as party nibblers or with a side salad as a meal for a family of four. If you want to turn up the heat on this tasty Mexican dish, try adding 1/4 cup of diced pickled jalapeno slices to your quesadillas. When preparing the quesadillas, add the jalapenos after adding the beans but before adding the rest of the cheese.

Makes 32 pieces

INGREDIENTS

8 6-inch whole wheat or flavored flour tortillas

2⅔ cups shredded cheddar blend, lightly packed

½ cup regular salsa or taco sauce

1 cup canned black or kidney beans, drained and rinsed

Cheesy Bean Quesadillas

Step 6

Step 8

1 Place a baking pan in the oven and preheat the oven to 250°F.

2 Place one tortilla on a piece of paper towel or waxed paper on the countertop.

3 Lightly pack a 1/3-cup dry measuring cup with cheese.

4 Sprinkle half of the cheese over the bottom half of the tortilla, spreading evenly to within 1/4 inch of the edge.

5 Spoon 1 tablespoon of salsa (or taco sauce) evenly over the cheese.

6 Place 2 tablespoons of the beans evenly over the salsa.

7 Sprinkle the remaining half of the 1/3 cup of cheese over the beans.

8 Fold the top half of the tortilla over the bottom half and press down slightly. Set aside.

9 Repeat steps 2 to 8 for the remaining tortillas.

10 Heat a large skillet over medium heat, about 2 minutes.

Can I prepare my quesadillas in advance?

You can prepare these quesadillas up to 24 hours in advance. Perform steps 2 to 9 below and then stack the prepared quesadillas in pairs and wrap them in plastic wrap. Keep them in the refrigerator until you're ready to cook and serve them. Keep in mind that if you are cooking the quesadillas when they are still cold from the refrigerator, they may take a bit longer to cook.

Nutrition Facts Per Piece	
Calories	71
Calories from Fat	34
Total Fat	4 g
Saturated Fat	2 g
Monounsaturated Fat	1 g
Polyunsaturated Fat	0 g
Cholesterol	10 mg
Sodium	129 mg
Total Carbohydrates	5 g
Dietary Fiber	1 g
Sugars	0 g
Protein	4 g

Steps 11 & 12

Step 14

11 Carefully place 2 folded tortillas, or quesadillas, into the skillet. Press down on the quesadillas with a spatula.

12 Cook until the bottoms of the quesadillas are lightly browned and crisp, about 2 to 3 minutes.

13 Using the spatula, carefully turn each quesadilla and cook on the second side until lightly browned and crisp, and the cheese inside is melted, about 2 to 3 minutes.

14 Place the quesadillas onto the baking pan in the oven to keep warm.

15 Repeat steps 11 to 14 for the remaining tortillas.

16 Remove the baking pan from the oven. Place the quesadillas on a cutting board.

17 Using a chef's knife, cut each quesadilla in half. Then cut each piece in half again to make four pieces.

• Quesadillas are delicious served with sour cream and salsa.

Roasted Red Pepper Spirals

These colorful spirals are sure to be a hit at your next social gathering. Your friends and family will think you spent all day making these delectable treats—only you will know the truth!

When purchasing goat cheese for this recipe, make sure you choose a soft goat cheese, which is usually sold in see-through tubes, rather than a hard goat cheese.

Makes 48 pieces

INGREDIENTS

1/2 cup drained roasted red peppers (packed in a jar), patted dry

4 whole wheat or flavored 10-inch flour tortillas

1/2 cup soft goat cheese or cream cheese, at room temperature

4 teaspoons honey Dijon mustard

2 tablespoons chiffonade (thin strips) of fresh basil (see page 99)

4 pinches of pepper

Roasted Red Pepper Spirals

1. Cut the red peppers into 1/4-inch strips and divide into 4 equal portions. Set aside.

2. Place one tortilla on a piece of waxed paper or paper towel.

3. Using a table knife, spread 2 tablespoons of goat (or cream) cheese evenly over the tortilla, leaving a 1/2-inch cheese-free border around the edge.

4. Using a pastry brush, spread 1 teaspoon of mustard evenly over the cheese.

5. Sprinkle 1/4 of the basil evenly over the cheese. Sprinkle with a pinch of pepper.

6. Place half of one portion of the red pepper strips in a single horizontal layer across the center of the tortilla.

7. Place the other half of the red pepper strips in a single horizontal layer across the bottom of the tortilla, about 1 inch from the bottom.

Tip

Are there any variations of this recipe that I can try?

For a stylish alternative, try smoked salmon spirals instead. Substitute 1/2 cup of smoked salmon for the roasted peppers, cream cheese for the goat cheese and 2 tablespoons of chopped chives or green onions for the basil. Leave out the honey Dijon mustard.

Nutrition Facts Per Piece	
Calories	14
Calories from Fat	4
Total Fat	0 g
Saturated Fat	0 g
Monounsaturated Fat	0 g
Polyunsaturated Fat	0 g
Cholesterol	1 mg
Sodium	33 mg
Total Carbohydrates	2 g
Dietary Fiber	0 g
Sugars	0 g
Protein	1 g

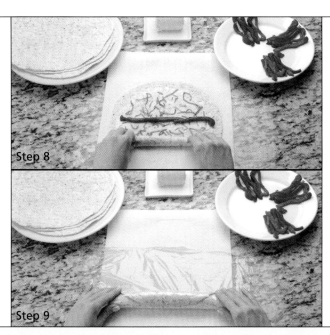

Step 8

Step 9

8 Starting at the bottom edge of the tortilla, roll up the tortilla as tightly as possible. Make sure to keep the red pepper strips from slipping upwards. Roll up completely.

9 Wrap the rolled-up tortilla in a sheet of plastic wrap.

10 Repeat steps 2 to 9 with the remaining tortillas. Refrigerate for at least 2 hours or overnight.

11 When you are ready to serve, remove one tortilla roll from the plastic wrap.

12 Using a sharp chef's knife, cut off the hollow ends of the tortilla on the diagonal and discard.

13 Cut the tortilla roll into 12 evenly-sized pieces on the diagonal.

Vegetable Bean Soup

This wholesome and nourishing Vegetable Bean Soup is a bowl of comfort on a cold winter afternoon. For a southwestern feast, try serving the soup along with small bowls of shredded cheddar or Monterey Jack cheese, sour cream, sliced green onions and crumbled tortilla chips.

Makes 8 servings

INGREDIENTS

2 cloves garlic, minced
1 tablespoon ground cumin
1/2 teaspoon ground coriander seed
1/2 teaspoon salt and 1/4 teaspoon pepper
2 tablespoons extra virgin olive oil
1 large onion, diced into 1/4-inch pieces
4 cups low-sodium chicken or vegetable broth
1 can (28 ounces) diced tomatoes
1 can (15 1/2 to 19 ounces) kidney beans, drained and rinsed
2 cups frozen mixed vegetables (do not thaw)

Vegetable Bean Soup

1 In a small bowl, combine the garlic, cumin, coriander, salt and pepper. Set aside.

2 Heat a large saucepan over medium heat for 1 to 2 minutes.

3 Add the oil to the pan and allow to heat up for about 20 seconds.

4 Place the onion in the saucepan and stir often until softened, about 5 minutes.

5 Add the garlic and seasoning mixture to the onion. Stir continuously for 1 minute.

6 Add the chicken (or vegetable) broth and diced tomatoes to the saucepan. Stir well.

How can I vary this soup recipe?

For a fast and easy minestrone soup, use 1 tablespoon of dried oregano leaves instead of the cumin and coriander. Then substitute 1 cup of frozen cut green beans and 1 cup of frozen sliced carrots for all of the mixed vegetables. For a heartier minestrone, you can add 1 cup of cooked pasta, such as macaroni, to the soup before serving. Then top the soup with grated parmesan cheese, allowing it to melt into the hot soup.

Nutrition Facts Per Serving	
Calories	177
Calories from Fat	42
Total Fat	5 g
Saturated Fat	1 g
Monounsaturated Fat	3 g
Polyunsaturated Fat	0 g
Cholesterol	0 mg
Sodium	535 mg
Total Carbohydrates	26 g
Dietary Fiber	7 g
Sugars	6 g
Protein	9 g

7 Increase the heat to bring the mixture to a boil.

8 Once the mixture is boiling, add the kidney beans and frozen vegetables to the mixture. Stir well and bring to a boil again.

9 Reduce the heat and simmer, allowing the mixture to gently bubble. Cover the saucepan with a lid.

10 Let the mixture simmer, stirring occasionally, for approximately 10 minutes.

11 Remove the saucepan from the heat and serve.

Butternut Squash Soup

This thick, tasty purée of butternut squash and pumpkin, delicately flavored with nutmeg and thyme, is perfect for dinner on a cool autumn evening. You can keep this Butternut Squash Soup refrigerated for 2 to 3 days after preparing it. Like many homemade soups, it tastes better the day after it's made.

Makes 8 servings

INGREDIENTS

2 tablespoons extra virgin olive oil
2 medium onions, diced into 1/4-inch pieces
3 medium carrots, chopped
2 celery stalks, chopped
1/4 teaspoon ground nutmeg
1/4 teaspoon dried thyme leaves
6 cups low-sodium vegetable or chicken broth
1 can (14 ounces) pure pumpkin, unsweetened
2 teaspoons salt and 1/4 teaspoon pepper
2 1/2 pounds frozen butternut squash pieces
(do not thaw)

Butternut Squash Soup

Step 4

1 Heat a large stockpot or saucepan over medium heat for 1 to 2 minutes.

2 Add the oil to the stockpot and heat up for about 20 seconds.

3 Place the onions in the stockpot and stir often until softened, about 5 minutes.

4 Add the carrots and celery to the stockpot and cook, stirring often, for about 5 minutes.

5 Add the nutmeg and thyme to the stockpot and stir to combine.

6 Add the vegetable (or chicken) broth, pumpkin, salt, pepper and frozen squash to the stockpot. Stir well to combine.

7 Increase the heat and bring the mixture to a boil.

Tip

Can I use a hand-held blender instead of a countertop blender?

Hand-held blenders can be faster, safer (no hot-liquid spills to worry about) and easier to clean up than countertop blenders. Instead of performing steps 10 and 11 below, simply use your hand-held blender to purée the soup directly in the stockpot. For information on hand-held blenders, known as immersion blenders, see page 25.

Nutrition Facts Per Serving	
Calories	181
Calories from Fat	45
Total Fat	5 g
Saturated Fat	1 g
Monounsaturated Fat	3 g
Polyunsaturated Fat	1 g
Cholesterol	0 mg
Sodium	665 mg
Total Carbohydrates	32 g
Dietary Fiber	5 g
Sugars	8 g
Protein	7 g

8 Reduce the heat and simmer, allowing the mixture to gently bubble. Cover the stockpot with a lid.

9 Let the mixture simmer, stirring occasionally, until the vegetables are tender, about 30 minutes.

10 Using a heat resistant ladle, transfer the mixture in small batches to a blender and purée until smooth.

11 Repeat step 10 until all of the mixture has been puréed.

12 Return the soup to the stockpot and simmer uncovered for another 10 minutes to allow the flavors to blend together.

• Try serving this soup with a heaping tablespoon of sour cream and a sprinkle of freshly ground nutmeg.

Asian Noodle Soup

This soup is packed with flavorful vegetables and lots of noodles. Instead of rice vermicelli, try other Asian noodles, such as fresh chow mein noodles, udon or soba noodles. You can also make this soup into a complete meal by adding 1/2 to 3/4 pound of protein, such as silken tofu or cooked chicken or shrimp. Add the protein to your soup after the broccoli is heated through and simmer until the tofu, chicken or shrimp is also heated through.

Makes 6 servings

INGREDIENTS

1 cup dried shiitake mushrooms
12 to 16 ounces dried rice vermicelli
6 cups low-sodium chicken or vegetable broth
2 cups Asian-style chicken broth
1 lime, cut in half widthwise
1 pound frozen broccoli spears or florets
3 stalks celery, sliced 1/4-inch thick on the diagonal
1 tablespoon toasted sesame oil
3 green onions, cut into 1/4-inch slices
1 1/2 cups fresh bean sprouts, washed and drained

Asian Noodle Soup

Step 5

Step 7

1 Add the dried shiitakes to a medium bowl. Add just enough boiling water so all the shiitakes barely float in the bowl. Set aside.

2 Prepare the rice vermicelli according to the package directions. Drain and set aside.

3 In a large stockpot, add all of the broth. Cover the pot and increase the heat to bring to a simmer, allowing the mixture to gently bubble.

4 Once the mixture is simmering, remove the lid from the pot.

5 Holding a medium fine mesh strainer over the pot, pour the water from the shiitakes into the pot, keeping the shiitakes in the strainer.

6 Place the shiitakes on a cutting board and, using a chef's knife, remove the tough stems and discard.

7 Slice the shiitakes into 1/4-inch slices and add them to the pot.

Can I use fresh vegetables instead of frozen?

Of course! Try using one pound of gai lan (also known as Chinese broccoli) instead of frozen broccoli. Add the whole stalks into the broth in step 10 below and cook until the stalks are tender but still firm, about 4 or 5 minutes. Gai lan is a tasty, healthy vegetable that is available in many supermarkets and Asian grocery stores.

Nutrition Facts Per Serving	
Calories	396
Calories from Fat	45
Total Fat	5 g
Saturated Fat	1 g
Monounsaturated Fat	1 g
Polyunsaturated Fat	1 g
Cholesterol	2 mg
Sodium	591 mg
Total Carbohydrates	66 g
Dietary Fiber	6 g
Sugars	2 g
Protein	18 g

8 Using a citrus reamer, squeeze the juice from both lime halves into the pot.

9 Stir the contents of the pot using a wooden spoon. Cover the pot and simmer for 10 minutes.

10 Add the frozen broccoli and the celery to the pot and increase the heat to bring to a boil. Reduce the heat and simmer uncovered until the broccoli is heated through, about 4 or 5 minutes.

11 Turn off the heat. Add the sesame oil and stir to combine.

12 Place the prepared rice vermicelli into 6 soup bowls. Ladle the soup over the vermicelli and top with the green onions and bean sprouts.

13 Serve with hoisin sauce and Asian chili paste or sriracha chili sauce for extra flavor. Provide each person with a set of chopsticks and a soup spoon.

Dressings & Marinades

Fat-Free Tomato

This tomato dressing is delicious over salad greens or as a marinade for chicken, beef or pork. Any unused dressing can be stored in a sealed container in the refrigerator for up to one week. When using this dressing as a marinade, discard the used portion after the food has finished marinating.

INGREDIENTS

1/2 cup tomato juice

1 tablespoon balsamic or sherry vinegar

1/2 teaspoon Dijon mustard

2 garlic cloves, minced

1/4 teaspoon salt and 1/8 teaspoon pepper

1/8 teaspoon hot sauce (optional)

1/8 teaspoon dried oregano leaves or Italian seasoning

---

1 In a small bowl, whisk the ingredients together until well blended.

• This recipe makes approximately 2/3 cup.

Asian

If you can't get enough of the grilled food at your favorite Asian restaurant, here is a mixture you can use as a salad dressing or marinade at home.

Let large cuts of meat marinate in this mixture overnight in the refrigerator. Marinate thinly sliced meats and poultry for no more than 2 hours and fish and seafood for no more than 30 minutes. Discard used marinade after the food has finished marinating.

INGREDIENTS

2 garlic cloves, minced

1 green onion, minced

1/4 cup rice vinegar

3 tablespoons Asian toasted sesame oil

2 tablespoons Asian fish sauce

2 tablespoons hoisin sauce

2 tablespoons granulated sugar

1/2 teaspoon Asian chili paste

1/2 teaspoon ground ginger

---

1 In a small bowl, whisk the ingredients together until well blended.

• This recipe makes approximately 1 cup.

• To add a peanut flavor to the dressing, add 1/4 cup creamy peanut butter to the ingredients above and stir until well blended.

Citrus

This citrus dressing is best served over delicate greens, such as leaf lettuce or baby spinach.

This mixture is also an ideal marinade for fish, seafood, poultry and meat. Fish and seafood should not marinate any longer than 30 minutes. Poultry and meat can marinate up to 24 hours. Discard the used marinade after the food has finished marinating.

INGREDIENTS

1 tablespoon Dijon mustard
2 tablespoons balsamic or sherry vinegar
1/8 teaspoon salt and 1/8 teaspoon pepper
1/3 cup extra virgin olive oil
3 tablespoons orange juice
1 teaspoon liquid honey

1. In a small bowl, add the Dijon mustard, vinegar, salt and pepper. Whisk well.

2. Slowly add the oil, whisking continuously until well blended.

3. Whisk in the orange juice and honey until blended.

- This recipe makes approximately 2/3 cup.

Indian

This virtually fat-free dressing is terrific tossed with steamed vegetables or as a marinade for chicken, fish or seafood. Because of the high acidic content of this mixture, you should marinate foods in a glass, stainless steel or ceramic bowl. Marinate chicken for at least 2 hours and fish and seafood for only 30 minutes. Discard the used marinade after the food has finished marinating.

INGREDIENTS

1 tablespoon ground coriander seed
1 1/2 teaspoons ground cumin
3 garlic cloves, minced
1 tablespoon freshly grated gingerroot
1 jalapeno pepper, seeded and minced
1 teaspoon salt
1/2 teaspoon turmeric
1/4 teaspoon ground cayenne pepper
1 cup plain nonfat yogurt
2 tablespoons fresh lemon juice

1. Heat a small skillet over medium heat for 1 to 2 minutes. Add the coriander and cumin to the skillet and cook, stirring continuously for 30 seconds.

2. Place the coriander and cumin in a medium bowl and add the rest of the ingredients. Whisk together until well blended.

- This recipe makes approximately 1 1/4 cups.

Summery Spinach Salad

Why make the same old tossed salad with bottled dressing when you can serve this beautiful, healthy, homemade alternative? Homemade vinaigrettes are always fresher tasting than store bought salad dressings and are free of unnecessary ingredients and preservatives.

Makes 4 servings

INGREDIENTS

$1/3$ cup pine nuts or slivered almonds

8 cups (6 ounce bag) baby spinach

$1/2$ small red onion, halved lengthwise and thinly sliced

$1/2$ cup drained canned mandarin orange segments, patted dry

$1/4$ cup plain low-fat yogurt

1 teaspoon Dijon mustard

2 tablespoons balsamic vinegar or sherry vinegar

1 pinch salt and 1 pinch pepper

Summery Spinach Salad

1 To toast the pine nuts (or almonds) you will sprinkle over the salad, heat a small skillet over medium heat for 1 to 2 minutes.

2 Add the pine nuts (or almonds) to the skillet and stir continuously until they are lightly browned, about 2 minutes.

3 Immediately place the pine nuts (or almonds) on a small plate to cool. Set aside.

4 Place the spinach, onion and orange segments in a large salad bowl.

Are there variations of the spinach salad that I can try?

You can vary the fruit and nuts in this salad or eliminate them entirely. Try using dried cranberries, dried cherries or slivered dried apricots instead of the orange segments. Instead of using pine nuts or slivered almonds, try using pecans or walnuts. Just remember to toast these nuts like we do for the pine nuts or almonds to bring out their natural oils and flavors. You can also try adding 4 ounces of blue cheese or goat cheese to the salad.

Nutrition Facts Per Serving	
Calories	119
Calories from Fat	72
Total Fat	8 g
Saturated Fat	1 g
Monounsaturated Fat	2 g
Polyunsaturated Fat	4 g
Cholesterol	1 mg
Sodium	67 mg
Total Carbohydrates	9 g
Dietary Fiber	2 g
Sugars	4 g
Protein	4 g

5 In a small bowl, add the yogurt, Dijon mustard, vinegar, salt and pepper.

6 Using a whisk, thoroughly blend the ingredients to create the salad dressing.

7 Just prior to serving, pour the dressing over the salad and toss gently with salad tongs.

8 Sprinkle the pine nuts (or almonds) over the salad and serve.

Classic Caesar Salad

The Classic Caesar Salad—made from scratch in your very own kitchen. This recipe calls for 8 cups of romaine lettuce, which is approximately 1 large head of lettuce. Instead of washing and tearing the lettuce yourself, you can save time by purchasing romaine lettuce that is pre-washed and already torn into bite-sized pieces.

Makes 4 servings

INGREDIENTS

8 cups romaine lettuce, torn into bite-sized pieces
2 cloves garlic, minced
2 tablespoons fresh lemon juice
1 tablespoon Dijon mustard
3 oil-packed anchovy fillets (in a jar or can), minced, or 1/4 teaspoon salt
1/4 teaspoon pepper
1/2 teaspoon Worcestershire sauce
1/4 cup extra virgin olive oil
4 tablespoons (1/4 cup) freshly grated parmesan cheese
1 cup croutons

Classic Caesar Salad

Step 1

Step 2

1 Place the romaine lettuce in a large salad bowl.

2 In a small bowl, combine the garlic, lemon juice, Dijon mustard, anchovies (or salt), pepper and Worcestershire sauce. Stir with a whisk until blended.

3 Place a dish towel or small rubber mat under the bowl to help prevent the bowl from moving.

4 Slowly pour the olive oil into the bowl, whisking continuously until the olive oil is blended well into the mixture.

5 Stir in 1 tablespoon of the grated parmesan cheese to complete the dressing.

How can I turn the Classic Caesar Salad into a main course?

You can easily turn the Classic Caesar Salad into a main course by adding protein to the salad, such as grilled chicken breast, steak or sautéed shrimp. Simply top each serving of salad with 3 to 4 ounces of protein to create a delicious meal.

Nutrition Facts Per Serving	
Calories	213
Calories from Fat	151
Total Fat	17g
Saturated Fat	3 g
Monounsaturated Fat	11 g
Polyunsaturated Fat	1 g
Cholesterol	8 mg
Sodium	354 mg
Total Carbohydrates	10 g
Dietary Fiber	1 g
Sugars	2 g
Protein	6 g

6 Just before serving, pour the dressing on top of the romaine lettuce in the salad bowl.

7 Add the croutons to the salad bowl and toss well with salad tongs to coat the lettuce and croutons with the dressing.

8 Sprinkle the remaining 3 tablespoons of parmesan cheese on top of the salad.

• Serve the salad immediately to keep the salad crisp.

Confetti Potato Salad

Tender boiled potatoes, crunchy red pepper and celery and zingy red wine vinegar—this potato salad is sure to please everyone, either at your own dinner table or at the next family picnic. For even more flavor, try topping your potato salad with some pitted black or green olives, or a seeded and diced jalapeno pepper.

Makes 4 servings

INGREDIENTS

1 1/2 pounds small new potatoes, scrubbed
2 tablespoons red wine or sherry vinegar
2 tablespoons extra virgin olive oil
1/2 teaspoon salt and 1/4 teaspoon pepper
2 tablespoons low fat mayonnaise (optional)
1 red pepper, diced into 1/4-inch pieces
1 stalk celery, diced into 1/4-inch pieces
2 green onions, sliced 1/4-inch thick widthwise

Confetti Potato Salad

1 Place the potatoes in a large saucepan and fill the saucepan with cold water to cover the potatoes by about 1 inch.

2 Place the saucepan over high heat and bring the water up to a boil.

3 Continue to boil the water until the potatoes are just tender when pierced with a paring knife, about 15 to 20 minutes.

Note: You may need to reduce the heat slightly to prevent the water from boiling over.

4 While the potatoes are boiling, add the vinegar, oil, salt, pepper and mayonnaise (if using) to a large bowl. Stir with a whisk until well blended.

5 Add the red pepper, celery and green onions to the large bowl. Stir with a whisk until combined.

How will I know when the potatoes are cooked?

Here's a surefire way to determine if your potatoes are cooked properly for potato salad. While the potatoes are boiling, insert a paring knife into the center of a potato and, holding the knife, slowly lift the potato out of the water. If the potato is cooked to just tender, the potato will slip off the knife as you lift it.

Nutrition Facts Per Serving	
Calories	225
Calories from Fat	78
Total Fat	9 g
Saturated Fat	1 g
Monounsaturated Fat	6 g
Polyunsaturated Fat	2 g
Cholesterol	2 mg
Sodium	361 mg
Total Carbohydrates	34 g
Dietary Fiber	5 g
Sugars	3 g
Protein	4 g

6 When the potatoes are just tender, drain into a large colander in the sink.

7 Using a paper towel to handle the hot potatoes, use a chef's knife to cut each potato into four pieces on a cutting board. When all of the potatoes are cut, add the potatoes to the large bowl.

8 Using salad tongs, toss well to combine the ingredients, making sure that the potatoes absorb all of the liquid.

• Serve the potato salad warm, at room temperature or chilled.

Savory Green Beans

Add a little spice to your dinner table with these delicious Savory Green Beans. When preparing this recipe, it is important to add the dressing to the green beans while the beans are still very hot. The heat from the beans helps to cook the minced garlic slightly. The heated combination of garlic, soy sauce and Dijon mustard creates a scrumptious dish.

Makes 4 servings

INGREDIENTS

1 tablespoon red wine vinegar
   or balsamic vinegar

1 tablespoon Dijon mustard

1¹/2 teaspoons soy sauce

2 cloves garlic, minced

¹/4 teaspoon pepper

1 tablespoon extra virgin olive oil

1 pound green beans, ends trimmed

Savory Green Beans

1 In a small bowl, mix together the vinegar, Dijon mustard, soy sauce, garlic and pepper with a whisk.

2 Pour the olive oil into the bowl, whisking continuously until the oil is blended into the mixture. Set aside.

3 In a large saucepan of boiling, salted water, cook the green beans until tender but still firm, about 4 to 5 minutes. Drain the green beans in a colander.

4 When drained, place the green beans into a large stainless steel or glass bowl.

Can I try this recipe with other vegetables instead of green beans?

Absolutely! You can use this flavorful dressing to spice up any steamed or boiled vegetable. For a bit of variety, try the dressing with steamed asparagus or broccoli. For information on steaming and boiling vegetables, see page 108. This dressing is also excellent drizzled over pan-fried fish, such as tilapia, or slices of grilled steak.

Nutrition Facts Per Serving	
Calories	73
Calories from Fat	34
Total Fat	4 g
Saturated Fat	1 g
Monounsaturated Fat	3 g
Polyunsaturated Fat	0 g
Cholesterol	0 mg
Sodium	217 mg
Total Carbohydrates	9 g
Dietary Fiber	3 g
Sugars	0 g
Protein	2 g

5 Pour the dressing from the small bowl over the green beans.

6 Using salad tongs, toss the green beans to thoroughly coat the beans with the dressing.

- Serve the green beans warm or at room temperature.

Broccoli Sauté

So easy and delicious, this Broccoli Sauté side dish is sure to become a favorite. Shocking the steamed broccoli in an ice bath stops the cooking process and allows the broccoli to keep its vivid green color and perfect texture.

Makes 4 servings

INGREDIENTS

1 bunch broccoli, cut into florets, stalks peeled and sliced

3 garlic cloves, thinly sliced

1/2 teaspoon salt and 1/4 teaspoon pepper

1/4 teaspoon red pepper flakes (optional)

2 tablespoons extra virgin olive oil

Broccoli Sauté

Step 2

1 In a large saucepan fitted with a steamer insert, steam the broccoli until the stalks are barely tender, about 4 minutes.

Note: For information on steaming, see page 106.

2 Fill a large bowl two-thirds full with cold water and several ice cubes. This will be used as an ice bath for the broccoli.

Note: For information on ice baths, see page 105.

3 Using tongs, remove the broccoli from the steamer insert and immediately add to the ice bath.

4 Chill the broccoli completely in the ice bath, about 1 to 2 minutes.

5 Remove the broccoli from the ice bath with tongs and place in a colander to drain. Set aside.

6 In a small bowl, combine the garlic, salt, pepper and red pepper flakes (if using). Set aside.

Can I try other vegetables in this recipe?

Absolutely! Try this recipe with asparagus, snow peas or any vegetable of your choice instead of broccoli. Just follow the steaming or boiling instructions on page 108 and away you go. For an extra dash of color and flavor, you can also try adding a few slices of roasted red pepper to the broccoli in step 10 below.

Nutrition Facts Per Serving	
Calories	119
Calories from Fat	68
Total Fat	8 g
Saturated Fat	1 g
Monounsaturated Fat	5 g
Polyunsaturated Fat	1 g
Cholesterol	0 mg
Sodium	341 mg
Total Carbohydrates	11 g
Dietary Fiber	4 g
Sugars	3 g
Protein	4 g

Step 9

Step 10

7 Heat a large skillet over medium heat for 1 to 2 minutes.

8 Add the oil to the skillet and allow to heat up for about 20 seconds.

9 Add the garlic mixture to the skillet and cook, stirring continuously, for 1 minute.

10 Add the broccoli to the skillet. Use two wooden spoons to toss the broccoli and coat with the garlic mixture.

11 Cook until the broccoli is heated through, about 2 to 3 minutes.

• Serve the broccoli warm or at room temperature.

Garlic Mushrooms

So quick! So easy! So delicious! These Garlic Mushrooms are delicious as prepared below, but you can also vary this recipe by trying out some more exotic mushrooms from the grocery store. This recipe is also great with sliced portobellos, oyster mushrooms, fresh shiitakes, or a combination of different types. Be careful not to slice the mushrooms too thin, as they shrink down during cooking.

Makes 4 servings

INGREDIENTS

2 cloves garlic, minced

1/2 teaspoon salt and 1/8 teaspoon pepper

2 tablespoons extra virgin olive oil

1 pound fresh white or brown (cremini) mushrooms, sliced 1/4-inch thick

1 tablespoon fresh lemon juice or balsamic vinegar (optional)

2 tablespoons finely chopped Italian parsley (optional)

Garlic Mushrooms

1 In a small bowl, combine the garlic, salt and pepper. Set aside.

2 Heat a large skillet or sauté pan over medium-high heat for 1 to 2 minutes.

3 Add the oil to the pan and allow to heat up for about 20 seconds.

4 Add the mushrooms to the pan. Use a wooden spoon to stir the mushrooms and coat with the oil.

5 Cook the mushrooms, stirring occasionally, until the mushrooms are cooked through and lightly browned, about 5 minutes.

Tip

Are there any variations of this recipe?

For a different flavor, try using herbs other than parsley, such as basil or cilantro. If you are using tougher-leaved herbs, like rosemary, or strongly flavored herbs, like tarragon, use them more sparingly than the milder Italian parsley.

Nutrition Facts Per Serving	
Calories	91
Calories from Fat	65
Total Fat	7 g
Saturated Fat	1 g
Monounsaturated Fat	5 g
Polyunsaturated Fat	1 g
Cholesterol	0 mg
Sodium	299 mg
Total Carbohydrates	5 g
Dietary Fiber	0 g
Sugars	3 g
Protein	2 g

6 Add the garlic mixture to the pan and cook, stirring continuously, for 1 minute.

7 Add the lemon juice or balsamic vinegar (if using), and stir.

8 Turn off the heat and stir in the parsley (if using). Serve immediately.

• These mushrooms are great served over The Perfect Steak shown on page 178.

Classic Rice Pilaf

Rice pilaf is an easy side dish that can add sophistication to any meal. You can easily double or triple this recipe to feed a crowd, but stick with only 2 bay leaves and do not use more than 1/4 cup of oil. The saucepan you use to make this rice pilaf dish must be able to go into the oven to finish cooking the dish. If your saucepan has a plastic handle and plastic lid knob, you can easily ovenproof the handle and knob by wrapping them with 2 or 3 layers of aluminum foil.

Makes 4 servings

INGREDIENTS

2 tablespoons extra virgin olive oil

1 shallot or 1/2 small onion, minced

1 cup long-grain brown rice or brown basmati rice

2 cups low-sodium chicken or vegetable broth

1/2 teaspoon dried thyme leaves

1/2 teaspoon turmeric or saffron

1/4 teaspoon pepper

2 bay leaves

Classic Rice Pilaf

1 Preheat the oven to 350°F.

2 Heat a large ovenproof saucepan over medium heat for 1 to 2 minutes.

3 Add the oil to the pan and heat up for about 20 seconds.

4 Add the shallot (or onion) and cook, stirring occasionally, for 1 minute.

5 Add the rice to the saucepan.

6 Stir to coat the rice with the oil and the shallot. Continue stirring until the rice becomes more opaque, about 1 to 2 minutes.

7 Add the broth to the saucepan. Be careful, as the broth may splatter and steam may rise from the pan.

Variations!

The beauty of this rice pilaf dish is that it can be varied in so many ways. Try adding 3 tablespoons of dried currants and 2 tablespoons of toasted pine nuts when you add the broth. For a delicate tomato flavor, add a peeled, seeded tomato, diced into 1/4-inch pieces, when you add the broth. To create a fragrant Indian dish, include a cinnamon stick, 3 whole cardamom pods, 1/3 cup of toasted slivered almonds, 2 tablespoons of dried currants and 1 teaspoon of cumin when you add the broth.

Nutrition Facts Per Serving	
Calories	259
Calories from Fat	82
Total Fat	9 g
Saturated Fat	1 g
Monounsaturated Fat	6 g
Polyunsaturated Fat	1 g
Cholesterol	0 mg
Sodium	40 mg
Total Carbohydrates	39 g
Dietary Fiber	2 g
Sugars	1 g
Protein	6 g

8 Add the thyme, turmeric (or saffron), pepper and bay leaves to the saucepan.

9 Stir very briefly to combine the ingredients and then increase the heat to bring the mixture to a boil.

10 Cover the saucepan and place in the oven.

11 Cook until the rice has absorbed all of the liquid, about 45 to 50 minutes.

12 Remove the saucepan from the oven and let the rice sit, covered, for 10 minutes.

13 Remove the lid from the saucepan and remove the bay leaves.

14 Fluff the rice with a fork and serve.

Mashed Potatoes

We've taken the guilt out of one of our most cherished comfort foods—mashed potatoes. These mashed potatoes are extremely low in fat for something so delicious and rich tasting. We've removed the traditional cream and replaced it with buttermilk, which is creamy but has only 1% butterfat content.

Makes 6 servings

INGREDIENTS

3 large (about 1 1/2 pounds) Yukon Gold or yellow flesh potatoes, cut into 1 1/2-inch chunks

1/2 cup buttermilk (shake carton well before using)

2/3 cup 1% milk, plus more if desired

1 tablespoon unsalted butter or unsalted margarine, plus more if desired

1 teaspoon salt and 1/8 teaspoon pepper, plus more if desired

Mashed Potatoes

1 Place the potato chunks in a large saucepan.

2 Fill the saucepan with cold water to cover the potato chunks by about 1 inch.

3 Heat the saucepan over high heat and bring the water to a boil.

4 Once the water is boiling, add 1 tablespoon of salt.

5 Continue to boil the water until the potatoes are tender when pierced with a paring knife, about 15 minutes.

• Adjust the burner temperature if necessary to make sure the water does not boil over.

6 Drain the potatoes in a large colander placed in the sink.

7 Return the potatoes to the empty saucepan. Place the saucepan on a cold burner on the stove.

How can I vary my mashed potatoes the next time I make them?

For a different taste with added vitamins and fiber, try this recipe with equal parts of Yukon Gold potatoes and rutabaga or sweet potatoes. Cut the rutabaga or sweet potatoes into chunks the same size as the potatoes. Continue with the recipe as directed, but add only one half of the buttermilk and the milk, adding more if desired. If you like, you can also stir in 1/2 teaspoon of freshly grated nutmeg. To peel and cut a rutabaga, follow the directions for preparing a melon on page 87.

Nutrition Facts Per Serving	
Calories	180
Calories from Fat	22
Total Fat	2 g
Saturated Fat	2 g
Monounsaturated Fat	0 g
Polyunsaturated Fat	0 g
Cholesterol	8 mg
Sodium	436 mg
Total Carbohydrates	35 g
Dietary Fiber	4 g
Sugars	4 g
Protein	5 g

8 Add the buttermilk, milk and butter (or margarine) to the saucepan.

9 Using a potato masher, mash the potatoes until you achieve the desired texture (lumpy or smooth).

10 Stir the potatoes with the potato masher to blend the ingredients.

11 Add the salt and pepper to the potatoes. Stir well using a rubber spatula or wooden spoon.

• If you would like the potatoes to have a creamier consistency, you can add more milk to the potatoes and repeat step 10.

• Add more salt and pepper if desired.

• These mashed potatoes are delicious served with the meatloaf shown on page 174.

Roasted Vegetables

This side dish is a sweet treat. Carrots, parsnips and sweet potatoes contain sugars which create an irresistible dish when roasted. After roasting, the carrots will remain firmer than the parsnips and sweet potatoes. If you prefer some of the vegetables to others, you can roast just one or two—simply use 1 1/2 pounds in total.

Makes 4 servings

INGREDIENTS

1/2 pound carrots, cut into 1-inch chunks

1/2 pound parsnips, cut into 1-inch chunks

1/2 pound sweet potatoes, cut into 1-inch chunks

2 tablespoons extra virgin olive oil

1/4 teaspoon dried thyme or oregano leaves

1 teaspoon salt

1 tablespoon balsamic or sherry vinegar (optional)

Roasted Vegetables

1 Preheat the oven to 425°F.

2 Cover the bottom of a 9x13 baking sheet with parchment paper.

3 In a large bowl, add the carrots, parsnips and sweet potatoes.

4 Add the oil, thyme (or oregano) and salt to the bowl.

5 Mix well with your hands to coat the vegetables with the oil and seasonings.

What other vegetables can I roast?

Try roasting beets along with the other vegetables in this recipe. Use fewer of the other vegetables so you maintain a total of 1 1/2 pounds of vegetables. To add beets to the recipe, peel and cut them into one-inch chunks. Toss the beets separately with some of the oil and seasonings and place them on a separate area of the baking sheet so their red color will not bleed into the other vegetables. Once cooked, toss all the vegetables together before serving.

Nutrition Facts Per Serving	
Calories	177
Calories from Fat	66
Total Fat	7 g
Saturated Fat	1 g
Monounsaturated Fat	5 g
Polyunsaturated Fat	1 g
Cholesterol	0 mg
Sodium	634 mg
Total Carbohydrates	27 g
Dietary Fiber	6 g
Sugars	9 g
Protein	2 g

6 Place the vegetables in a single layer on the prepared baking sheet.

7 Place the baking sheet in the oven to roast, about 35 to 45 minutes.

• Roast until the sweet potatoes are soft and the carrots and parsnips are tender but still slightly firm when pierced with a paring knife.

8 Using a spatula, place the vegetables into a serving bowl or platter.

9 Add the balsamic (or sherry) vinegar, if using, and toss the vegetables with salad tongs to coat with the vinegar.

• Serve warm or at room temperature.

Roasted Potato Wedges

These golden brown potato wedges are so tender and flavorful, they barely make it from the baking pan to the serving dish. In our recipe, we use unpeeled potatoes. Feel free to use peeled potatoes if you prefer.

Makes 4 servings

INGREDIENTS

4 large Yukon gold or russet potatoes

2 teaspoons garlic powder

1 teaspoon paprika

1 teaspoon dry mustard

1 teaspoon salt and $1/4$ teaspoon pepper

$1/2$ teaspoon dried rosemary or thyme leaves

$1/4$ teaspoon sugar

$1/4$ cup water

2 tablespoons extra virgin olive oil

Roasted Potato Wedges

Step 3

Steps 4 & 5

Step 6

1 Preheat the oven to 425°F.

2 Cover the bottom of a 9x13 baking sheet or baking pan with parchment paper.

3 To cut a potato into wedges, cut the potato in half lengthwise using a chef's knife.

4 Place each half of the potato cut side down.

5 Cut each half of the potato lengthwise to create 4 wedges.

6 Cut each potato wedge lengthwise to create 8 wedges.

7 Repeat steps 3 to 6 with the remaining potatoes. Each potato will create 8 wedges.

Are there any variations of this recipe?

You can easily create your own variations on this dish by trying different flavorings. For example, for a Greek twist on this dish, try using 1/2 teaspoon of oregano instead of the rosemary or thyme, and whisk in the juice of half a lemon with the olive oil.

Nutrition Facts Per Serving	
Calories	358
Calories from Fat	68
Total Fat	8 g
Saturated Fat	1 g
Monounsaturated Fat	5 g
Polyunsaturated Fat	1 g
Cholesterol	0 mg
Sodium	646 mg
Total Carbohydrates	67 g
Dietary Fiber	9 g
Sugars	4 g
Protein	8 g

8 In a small bowl, mix together the garlic powder, paprika, dry mustard, salt, pepper, rosemary (or thyme) and sugar with a whisk.

9 In a large bowl, add the potato wedges. Pour 1/4 cup of water over the potato wedges.

10 Pour the oil and seasoning mixture over the potatoes in the large bowl.

11 With your hands, toss the potato wedges to coat with the oil and the seasoning mixture.

12 Place the potato wedges in a single layer on the prepared pan and drizzle any remaining seasoning liquid left in the bowl over the potatoes.

13 Bake until the potatoes are tender and golden brown, about 35 to 40 minutes.

14 Remove from the oven and serve immediately. These potato wedges are also delicious served at room temperature.

Vegetable & Cheese Omelet

Use this recipe to ensure that your omelets will be light, fluffy and delicious from now on. This recipe uses 2 eggs per omelet, but you can use 3 eggs if you prefer.

For the best omelets, before starting this recipe, place the eggs with their shell on into a large bowl and add hot tap water to cover the eggs. Let the eggs sit in the water for 4 minutes and then remove.

Makes 2 omelets

INGREDIENTS

1 tablespoon extra virgin olive oil

1/2 small onion, halved and thinly sliced

1 cup frozen mixed vegetables

1/8 teaspoon Italian seasoning or dried oregano leaves

1/8 teaspoon salt and 1/8 teaspoon pepper

4 eggs

2 tablespoons butter

1/4 cup grated cheddar or Swiss cheese

Vegetable & Cheese Omelet

Steps 5 & 6

Step 8

1 Heat a large skillet over medium heat, about 1 to 2 minutes.

2 Add the oil to the skillet and heat up for about 20 seconds.

3 Place the onion in the skillet and stir often until softened, about 5 minutes.

4 Turn the heat to medium high and add the vegetables, Italian seasoning (or oregano), salt and pepper. Cook until the vegetables are heated through, about 2 to 5 minutes. Place the vegetables into a bowl and set aside.

5 Break 2 eggs into a small bowl. Lightly beat the eggs with a fork.

6 Heat a small skillet over medium-low heat, about 1 to 2 minutes.

7 Add 1 tablespoon of butter to the skillet and swirl the skillet to coat its surface.

8 Add the beaten eggs to the skillet. Allow the eggs to sit in the skillet until they have solidified on the bottom, about 1 minute.

Tip

Are there other fillings that I can try in my omelets?

The variety of fillings you can use in omelets is almost endless. Try some of the following filling ideas instead of the mixed vegetables and cheddar cheese shown in the recipe below.

✓ 2/3 cup sautéed mushrooms and 1/4 cup grated Swiss cheese.

✓ 2/3 cup smoked salmon, 2 tablespoons chopped green onions and 1/4 cup crumbled soft goat cheese.

✓ 1/2 cup diced ham, 1/2 cup diced cooked potatoes or bell pepper and 1/4 cup grated cheddar cheese.

Nutrition Facts Per Omelet	
Calories	395
Calories from Fat	284
Total Fat	32 g
Saturated Fat	14 g
Monounsaturated Fat	13 g
Polyunsaturated Fat	2 g
Cholesterol	416 mg
Sodium	453 mg
Total Carbohydrates	10 g
Dietary Fiber	3 g
Sugars	4 g
Protein	16 g

9 Place a heatproof rubber spatula under the edge of the eggs, gently pushing towards the center of the skillet.

10 Continue performing step 9 for 2 to 3 minutes, moving in a circle around the skillet, until just a small amount of wet egg still remains on the surface.

11 Remove the skillet from the burner.

12 Spoon half of the cheese and half of the vegetable mixture evenly onto one half of the omelet.

13 Using a heatproof rubber spatula, fold the other half of the omelet over the filling.

14 Using the spatula, carefully slide the omelet onto a plate and serve.

15 Repeat steps 5 to 14 for the remaining 2 eggs and the other half of the cheese and vegetable mixture.

Fried & Scrambled Eggs

Once you learn the proper techniques for frying and scrambling eggs, your eggs will turn out perfectly every time. As a rule of thumb, you should avoid frying eggs in extra virgin olive oil, since its strong flavor may overpower the eggs.

Sunny-side up eggs are fried on one side only. The trick to cooking these eggs is getting the yolks cooked to the desired degree of firmness without overcooking the whites. When making sunny-side up eggs, you should break each egg into its own bowl before adding it to the skillet so you can discard any eggs that have gone bad or have broken yolks.

Scrambling is a method of preparing eggs in which the white and yolk are blended together and then cooked in a skillet. Adding a small amount of water or milk to the blended eggs will make your scrambled eggs fluffier.

Fried Eggs - Sunny-Side Up

Step 4

1 Break two eggs, each into its own small bowl. Be careful not to break the yolks.

2 Heat a large skillet over medium-low heat for 2 minutes.

3 Add 1 tablespoon of olive oil and 1 tablespoon of butter to the skillet. Then swirl the skillet until the butter is melted and combined with the olive oil.

4 Holding a bowl close to the bottom of the skillet, slowly tip an egg into one side of the skillet. Repeat for the second egg on the opposite side of the skillet.

5 Cover with a lid and allow the eggs to cook for 2 minutes.

6 Remove the lid and gently touch a yolk with your fingertip to check for firmness and make sure it is no longer cold. The egg whites should be solid.

7 If the yolk is cooked to the desired firmness, use a wide spatula to carefully remove each egg from the skillet.

• If the yolk is not done, cover with a lid and continue to cook the eggs, checking for doneness every 30 seconds.

Tip

Is there another type of fried eggs?

Over-easy eggs are fried eggs that are flipped once the egg white and yolk have firmed up a bit. Perform steps 1 to 5 on page 160. Remove the lid from the skillet and slide a wide spatula under the center of one egg and its yolk. Carefully flip the egg over to complete the cooking process on the yolk side. Flip the other egg and then cook the eggs uncovered until they reach the desired firmness.

Scrambled Eggs

Step 7

Step 8

1 Break the desired number of eggs into a bowl. Allow two eggs per person.

2 Add 1 tablespoon of 1% milk or water to the bowl for every two eggs.

3 Using a whisk, gently beat the eggs and liquid until just blended. Do not over-beat the egg mixture.

4 Heat a large skillet over medium heat for 2 minutes.

5 Add 1 tablespoon of butter to the skillet. Then swirl the skillet until the butter is melted.

6 Pour the egg mixture into the skillet and allow the eggs to cook for 30 seconds.

7 Using a wooden spoon, slowly stir the eggs to create small lumps, or curds. Continue stirring slowly until the eggs are only slightly runny.

8 Remove the skillet from the heat and continue to stir the eggs until they reach the desired degree of doneness.

Fettuccine Alfredo

There is, perhaps, no pasta dish more decadent than Fettuccine Alfredo. For best results, use the small holes of your grater to get the Parmigiano cheese finely grated and, when adding the cheese to the sauce, keep stirring until the cheese is completely melted.

Egg fettuccine noodles often come in the form of nests. These look like small bird's nests, but loosen and separate into individual pasta strands as they cook.

Makes 6 servings

INGREDIENTS

2 tablespoons extra virgin olive oil
1 shallot or 1/2 small onion, minced
1 cup heavy (35%) cream
1/4 teaspoon pepper
1/2 cup (1 stick) unsalted butter, cut into 1/2-inch cubes
12 ounces egg fettuccine or tagliatelle nests
1/3 cup pasta cooking water, plus more, if needed
1 cup Parmigiano Reggiano cheese, finely grated
2 tablespoons finely chopped Italian parsley (optional)

Fettuccine Alfredo

Stockpot

Sauté pan

Step 5

Step 7

1 Bring a covered stockpot two-thirds filled with cold water to a boil. Keep at a boil until ready to use.

2 Heat a large sauté pan over medium heat for 2 minutes.

3 Add the oil and shallot to the pan and stir with a wooden spoon for 1 minute.

4 Add the cream to the pan and stir with a wooden spoon to blend.

5 Add the pepper and butter to the pan and stir until the butter is melted.

6 Increase the heat to medium high and allow to cook, stirring occasionally, for one minute. Turn off the heat.

7 Add 1 tablespoon of salt to the stockpot of boiling water and then add the pasta. Stir and separate the nests into long strands, for about one minute.

8 Boil the pasta until just barely al dente (see page 110), about 5 minutes.

Tip

Why do I need to add the pasta cooking water to the sauce?

The starch in the pasta cooking water helps the sauce stick to the noodles, so the two stay together as one when served. The starchy pasta cooking water also helps to enhance the creaminess of the Alfredo sauce without adding any extra calories.

Nutrition Facts Per Serving	
Calories	613
Calories from Fat	375
Total Fat	42 g
Saturated Fat	23 g
Monounsaturated Fat	14 g
Polyunsaturated Fat	2 g
Cholesterol	161 mg
Sodium	73 mg
Total Carbohydrates	44 g
Dietary Fiber	2 g
Sugars	2 g
Protein	16 g

9 Turn off the heat. Using a glass measuring cup, remove about 2/3 cup of pasta cooking water from the stockpot and set aside.

10 Drain the pasta into a large colander in the sink. Do not shake off the excess water.

11 Add the pasta and about 1/3 cup of the reserved pasta cooking water to the cream sauce and turn the heat on to medium high.

12 Using tongs or two wooden spoons, toss the pasta with the sauce until well combined, about 1 minute.

• To make the pasta creamier, you can add more pasta water as you toss the pasta.

13 Turn off the heat and add 1 cup of grated Parmigiano cheese and toss well.

14 Add in the parsley (if using) and toss well to combine.

• Serve the pasta with a sprinkle of freshly grated Parmigiano cheese.

Spinach-Stuffed Pasta Shells

You and your guests will love this delectable cheese-laden pasta dish. In addition to the reduced-fat ricotta cheese, feel free to use lower fat versions of the other cheeses in this recipe as well. Make sure you use jumbo pasta shells for this recipe. You won't be able to stuff smaller sized shells.

Makes 6 servings

INGREDIENTS

1/2 pound jumbo pasta shells (about 30 shells)
1 package (10 ounces) frozen chopped spinach or broccoli, cooked
1 jar (26 ounces) pasta sauce
16 ounces part-skim ricotta cheese
1/4 pound (about 1 cup) shredded cheddar or mozzarella cheese
1/2 teaspoon ground nutmeg
1 teaspoon salt and 1/4 teaspoon pepper
2 eggs
1/4 pound (about 1 cup) shredded mozzarella cheese or mozzarella blend

Spinach-Stuffed Pasta Shells

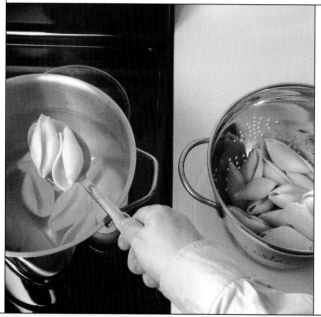

1 Preheat the oven to 350°F and lightly coat the inside of a 9x13 inch baking pan with oil.

2 Cook the pasta shells (see page 110). Using a slotted spoon, remove the shells and place them in a colander that is sitting on a plate.

3 Rinse the pasta shells under cold running water and set aside.

4 Gently squeeze the excess moisture from the cooked spinach (or broccoli) with your hands. Set aside.

5 Spread 1 1/4 cups of pasta sauce evenly over the bottom of the baking pan.

6 In a large bowl, place the spinach, ricotta cheese, shredded cheddar (or mozzarella), nutmeg, salt and pepper.

7 Break the eggs into a small bowl and then add to the spinach mixture. Stir well to combine.

Tip

How can I check the doneness of the pasta shells when they are cooking?

While cooking the pasta shells, use a slotted spoon to remove one shell from the pot. Run the shell under cold water for a few seconds and then open the shell with your fingers. If it opens easily, the shells are ready, but if it starts to tear, return it to the pot and cook for another minute. Keep checking every minute until the shells are done.

Nutrition Facts Per Serving	
Calories	451
Calories from Fat	173
Total Fat	19 g
Saturated Fat	11 g
Monounsaturated Fat	5 g
Polyunsaturated Fat	1 g
Cholesterol	120 mg
Sodium	1419 mg
Total Carbohydrates	44 g
Dietary Fiber	5 g
Sugars	8 g
Protein	28 g

Step 8

Step 11

8 Holding a pasta shell open in one hand, spoon 1 heaping tablespoon of filling into the pasta shell. Place into the baking pan.

9 Repeat step 8 with the remaining pasta shells.

10 Slowly pour the rest of the pasta sauce evenly over the pasta shells.

11 Sprinkle the mozzarella (or mozzarella blend) evenly over the entire surface of the baking pan.

12 Cover the pan loosely with aluminum foil.

13 Bake until the sauce is bubbling gently, about 20 to 25 minutes.

14 Remove the aluminum foil.

15 Bake until the top layer of the cheese is melted and the sauce is bubbling more vigorously, about 10 to 15 minutes.

• Try serving this dish with the Caesar Salad on page 140.

Old Fashioned Spaghetti & Meat Sauce

What is better than a steaming bowl of spaghetti and meat sauce? Eating it at home, knowing you made it from scratch! For a sauce with a bit more oomph, stir 1/2 cup of red wine into the cooked onions in step 5 below and cook for about one minute before proceeding with the rest of the recipe. Try serving this easy pasta dish topped with some freshly grated parmesan cheese, and some red pepper flakes if you want to add some heat.

Makes 6 servings

INGREDIENTS

1 tablespoon extra virgin olive oil
2 pounds lean ground beef or turkey
2 medium onions, diced into ¼-inch pieces
3 cloves garlic, minced
1 can (5½ ounces) tomato paste, plus 1 can water
1 can (28 ounces) whole tomatoes
1 tablespoon Italian seasoning or dried oregano leaves
2 teaspoons salt and ½ teaspoon pepper
2 bay leaves
1½ pounds spaghetti or linguini

Old Fashioned Spaghetti & Meat Sauce

1. Heat a large sauté pan over medium-high heat for 1 to 2 minutes.

2. Add the oil to the pan and allow to heat up for about 20 seconds.

3. Add the ground beef (or turkey) to the pan. Cook the meat, breaking it up with a wooden spoon and stirring occasionally, until there is no hint of pink remaining in the meat, about 8 to 10 minutes.

4. Reduce the heat to medium.

5. Add the onions to the meat and cook, stirring often with a clean wooden spoon until the onions are softened, about 5 minutes.

6. Add the garlic, tomato paste, can of water and whole tomatoes, breaking up the tomatoes with the edge of a clean wooden spoon.

Tip

Can I make a vegetarian sauce?

To create a delicious vegetarian version of this dish, heat a large sauté pan over medium heat and add 2 tablespoons of oil to the pan. Perform steps 5 to 9 below, but let the dish simmer for only 30 minutes. Then add 2 packages (24 ounces) of soy-based ground beef substitute, stir, and let cook for an additional 10 minutes. Then continue with steps 10 to 12.

Nutrition Facts Per Serving	
Calories	822
Calories from Fat	225
Total Fat	25 g
Saturated Fat	9 g
Monounsaturated Fat	11 g
Polyunsaturated Fat	2 g
Cholesterol	90 mg
Sodium	1066 mg
Total Carbohydrates	99 g
Dietary Fiber	6 g
Sugars	9 g
Protein	47 g

7 Add the Italian seasoning (or oregano), salt, pepper and bay leaves. Stir until the mixture is thoroughly combined. Bring to a boil.

8 Reduce the heat and simmer, allowing the mixture to gently bubble. Partially cover the sauté pan with a lid.

9 Let the mixture simmer, stirring occasionally, until the meat is tender and most of the liquid has been absorbed, about 40 minutes.

10 Turn off the heat, remove the lid and allow the sauce to sit for approximately 10 minutes. Remove the bay leaves.

• If necessary, use a spoon to skim off any fat from the surface of the meat sauce.

11 Cook the pasta. For information on cooking pasta, see page 110.

12 Serve the sauce with the pasta.

Hearty Chickpea Curry

If you are looking for a delicious vegetarian main course, try serving this Hearty Chickpea Curry with rice and a side salad. It is also great served as a side dish for 8 people or on a buffet table, hot or cold. Your vegetarian (and non-vegetarian) friends will thank you for it!

Makes 4 servings

INGREDIENTS

2 garlic cloves, minced
1 tablespoon mild or medium curry powder or paste
1 teaspoon ground cumin
2 tablespoons extra virgin olive oil
2 medium onions, diced into 1/4-inch pieces
1 can (28 ounces) diced tomatoes
2 cans (15 to 19 ounces each) chickpeas, drained and rinsed
3 medium carrots, sliced 1/8-inch thick
1 teaspoon salt and 1/4 teaspoon pepper
1 large green pepper, diced into 1/2-inch pieces

Hearty Chickpea Curry

Step 1
Steps 2 to 4

1 In a small bowl, combine the garlic, curry powder (or paste) and cumin. Set aside.

2 Heat a large saucepan or sauté pan over medium heat until hot, about 1 to 2 minutes.

3 Add the oil to the pan and heat up for about 20 seconds.

4 Place the onions in the pan and stir often until softened, about 5 minutes.

5 Add the garlic and curry mixture to the onions. Stir continuously for 1 minute.

6 Add the tomatoes, chickpeas, carrots, salt and pepper to the mixture. Stir until thoroughly combined.

7 Increase the heat to medium-high and bring the mixture to a boil.

Can I make this recipe with meat?

Of course! For a meaty alternative, start the recipe by cooking 1 pound of lean ground beef in 1 tablespoon of extra virgin olive oil in the pan over medium-high heat, until the meat is no longer pink. Then add the onions directly to the meat in the pan and proceed with the recipe, omitting 1 can of chickpeas.

Nutrition Facts Per Serving	
Calories	504
Calories from Fat	118
Total Fat	13 g
Saturated Fat	2 g
Monounsaturated Fat	7 g
Polyunsaturated Fat	3 g
Cholesterol	0 mg
Sodium	1676 mg
Total Carbohydrates	80 g
Dietary Fiber	20 g
Sugars	21 g
Protein	22 g

8 Once the mixture is boiling, reduce the heat and simmer, allowing the mixture to gently bubble. Cover the pan with a lid.

9 Let the mixture simmer, stirring occasionally, until the carrots are still slightly firm but can be pierced with a fork, about 20 minutes.

10 Remove the cover, stir in the green pepper and continue to cook uncovered until the green pepper is still slightly firm but can be pierced with a fork, about 5 minutes.

11 Remove the pan from the heat and serve.

Pan-Roasted Vegetables with Bulgur

If you are unfamiliar with bulgur, don't let that stop you from trying this delicious, satisfying dish. Bulgur's chewy texture and the sweet flavors of the roasted vegetables make this meat-free recipe a tantalizing main course or side dish. For an extra flavor dimension, try topping the dish with crumbled feta or blue cheese.

Makes 4 servings

INGREDIENTS

1 cup bulgur
1 teaspoon salt
1 batch Fat-Free Tomato Marinade & Dressing (see page 136)
3 tablespoons extra virgin olive oil
1 medium onion, halved and cut into ¹/₂-inch slices
1 large red pepper, cut into 1-inch chunks
1 large yellow, green or orange pepper, cut into 1-inch chunks
2 zucchinis, halved lengthwise and cut into ³/₄-inch chunks
2 tablespoons balsamic or sherry vinegar
1 can (15 to 19 ounces) bean medley, drained and rinsed

Pan-Roasted Vegetables with Bulgur

Step 1

Step 2

Step 8

1 Place the bulgur, salt and 3 cups of boiling water in a large bowl and stir gently. Cover the bowl with a large plate and set aside until the bulgur is almost soft, about 10 to 15 minutes.

2 Drain the bulgur into a fine mesh strainer, pressing gently with the back of a spoon to remove the excess water.

3 Place the bulgur back into the large bowl and stir with a fork.

4 Pour the dressing over the bulgur and stir well. Set aside.

5 Heat a large sauté pan over medium-high heat for 2 minutes.

6 Add 2 tablespoons of the oil to the pan and heat up for about 20 seconds. Carefully swirl the pan to coat the surface of the pan with the oil.

7 Add the onion and peppers to the pan in a single layer. Cook, without stirring, for 2 minutes.

8 Using two wooden spoons, toss the vegetables well and then cook for 2 minutes, stirring occasionally.

Tip

What is bulgur?

Bulgur, sometimes called burghul, is an extremely nutritious whole-grain product made from wheat that has been partially cooked, dried and ground. Bulgur, not to be confused with cracked wheat, is a main ingredient in the popular Middle Eastern salad, tabbouleh. In the recipe below, you can replace the bulgur with couscous, rice or wheat berries—just follow the package directions for preparing them.

Nutrition Facts Per Serving	
Calories	381
Calories from Fat	110
Total Fat	12 g
Saturated Fat	2 g
Monounsaturated Fat	8 g
Polyunsaturated Fat	2 g
Cholesterol	0 mg
Sodium	1086 mg
Total Carbohydrates	58 g
Dietary Fiber	15 g
Sugars	11 g
Protein	13 g

Step 9

Step 11

9 Place the onion and peppers in a medium bowl and set aside.

10 Add 1 tablespoon of oil to the pan.

11 Repeat steps 7 to 9 with the zucchini. Add the zucchini to the medium bowl with the other vegetables.

12 Immediately add the vinegar to the medium bowl and toss well with a serving spoon to coat all of the vegetables.

13 Add the beans to the large bowl of bulgur and combine using the serving spoon.

14 Serve the pan-roasted vegetables over the bulgur and bean mixture.

Come Back For More Chili

This recipe makes up a batch of delicious, Come Back for More Chili, with a medium-hot heat level. To make a milder chili, use only 1 teaspoon of ancho chili powder, or turn up the heat with a few dashes of your favorite hot sauce. Try serving this chili on a bed of mixed salad greens, onions and tomatoes, and top it with crumbled tortilla strips and sour cream.

Makes 4 servings

INGREDIENTS

4 garlic cloves, minced
2 teaspoons ground cumin
1 1/2 teaspoons ancho chili powder
1/2 teaspoon salt and 1/4 teaspoon pepper
1 tablespoon extra virgin olive oil
1 pound extra lean ground beef or ground turkey
2 small onions, diced into 3/4-inch pieces
1 small can (8 ounces) tomato sauce
1 cup low-sodium beef or vegetable broth
1 can (15 to 19 ounces) kidney or pinto beans, drained and rinsed

Come Back For More Chili

Step 4

Step 6

1 In a small bowl, combine the garlic, cumin, ancho chili powder, salt and pepper with a fork. Set aside.

2 Heat a large sauté pan over medium-high heat, about 2 minutes.

3 Add the oil to the pan and allow to heat up for about 20 seconds.

4 Add the ground beef (or turkey) to the pan. Cook the meat, breaking it up with a wooden spoon and stirring occasionally, until there is no hint of pink remaining in the meat, about 8 to 10 minutes.

5 Reduce the heat to medium.

6 Add the onions to the meat and cook, stirring often with a clean wooden spoon until the onions are softened, about 5 minutes.

Tip

What is ancho chili powder?

Ancho chili powder is one of many varieties of chili powder. Unlike regular chili powder, which is a blend of various chili peppers, cumin, oregano, salt and dehydrated garlic, the only ingredient in ancho chili powder is dried, smoked poblano chilies. This pure chili powder with a hint of smoky sweetness can make all the difference between regular chili and Come Back For More Chili.

Nutrition Facts Per Serving	
Calories	360
Calories from Fat	120
Total Fat	13 g
Saturated Fat	4 g
Monounsaturated Fat	7 g
Polyunsaturated Fat	1 g
Cholesterol	62 mg
Sodium	1061 mg
Total Carbohydrates	28 g
Dietary Fiber	6 g
Sugars	5 g
Protein	32 g

7 Add the garlic mixture and cook, stirring continuously for 1 minute.

8 Add the tomato sauce, beef (or vegetable) broth and kidney (or pinto) beans. Stir until the mixture is thoroughly combined. Bring to a boil.

9 Reduce the heat and simmer, allowing the mixture to gently bubble. Cover the sauté pan with a lid.

10 Let the mixture simmer, stirring occasionally, until the chili has thickened and the flavors have blended together, about 40 minutes.

11 Turn off the heat, remove the lid and allow the chili to sit for approximately 10 minutes.

• If necessary, use a spoon, to skim off any fat from the surface of the chili.

• Try serving this chili with the cornbread shown on page 212 and the spinach salad shown on page 138.

Melt In Your Mouth Meatloaf

Like a warm blanket on a cold night, meatloaf is all about comfort. This recipe is a down-home classic—simple to make and a treat to eat. The secret is the second coating of tomato sauce applied halfway through the cooking time. It creates a delightfully sticky top layer that is sure to please.

Makes 4 servings

INGREDIENTS
1 tablespoon extra virgin olive oil
1 small onion, diced into 1/4-inch pieces
2 eggs
1/2 cup plain dry bread crumbs
1 tablespoon garlic powder
1/2 teaspoon dried thyme leaves
1/4 teaspoon ground cayenne
2 tablespoons sweet relish
3/4 cup tomato sauce or pasta sauce
1 1/2 pounds extra lean ground beef or turkey

Melt In Your Mouth Meatloaf

1 Preheat the oven to 350°F.

2 Heat a small skillet over medium heat until hot, about 1 to 2 minutes.

3 Add the oil to the skillet and allow to heat up for about 20 seconds.

4 Place the onion in the skillet and stir often until softened, about 5 minutes. Place in a small bowl to cool and set aside.

5 In a large stainless steel or glass bowl, add the eggs, bread crumbs, garlic powder, thyme, cayenne, relish, 1/2 cup of the tomato (or pasta) sauce and the cooked onion. Stir with a whisk until well combined.

6 Add the ground beef (or turkey) to the large bowl. Mix the ingredients with your hands to combine, just until blended.

Tip

What can I do with leftover meatloaf?

Meatloaf is great in sandwiches. Just refrigerate the leftover meatloaf and later slice it up to any thickness you like. Pile the meatloaf onto some slices of fresh bread and add your favorite toppings. Meatloaf also freezes well after it has been cooked and cooled. Just wrap it in a double layer of aluminum foil before freezing. After thawing in the fridge, the meatloaf can be reheated in a 350°F oven until it is heated through, about 20 minutes.

Nutrition Facts Per Serving	
Calories	354
Calories from Fat	120
Total Fat	13 g
Saturated Fat	3 g
Monounsaturated Fat	7 g
Polyunsaturated Fat	1 g
Cholesterol	183 mg
Sodium	537 mg
Total Carbohydrates	19 g
Dietary Fiber	2 g
Sugars	4 g
Protein	39 g

7 Spoon the mixture into a 9x5x3 loaf pan, patting the mixture down with the back of a spoon as you place the mixture in the pan. Smooth out the top with the back of the spoon.

8 Place 2 tablespoons of the remaining tomato (or pasta) sauce on top of the meatloaf.

9 Using a pastry brush, brush the sauce evenly over the top.

10 Place the meatloaf in the oven and bake for 30 minutes.

11 Remove from the oven and brush the remaining sauce on top of the meatloaf.

12 Place the meatloaf back in the oven and bake until the center of the top of the meatloaf is firm, about 25 to 30 minutes.

• A meat thermometer inserted into the center of the meatloaf will register 160°F when the meatloaf is done.

13 Let the meatloaf stand for 10 minutes before slicing.

• Try serving the meatloaf with the mashed potatoes shown on page 152.

Simply the Best Beef Stew

Simply the Best Beef Stew is great to cook on a Sunday afternoon. It takes some time to prepare, but the end result is well worth it. If you have any leftovers, they'll taste even better the next day! The red lentils are the secret ingredient in this recipe. They melt away, making the sauce thick and luscious.

Makes 6 servings

INGREDIENTS

2 teaspoons salt and 1 teaspoon pepper

2^{1}/$_{2}$ pounds beef stew meat, in 1^{1}/$_{2}$- to 2-inch chunks, patted dry

2 tablespoons extra virgin olive oil (plus more if needed)

2 medium onions, diced into ^{1}/$_{4}$-inch pieces

4 large carrots, cut in half lengthwise, each half cut into 2-inch lengths

2 tablespoons tomato paste

1^{1}/$_{2}$ cups beer or red wine

2 cups low-sodium beef or chicken broth

^{1}/$_{3}$ cup dried red lentils

4 large red-skinned potatoes, cut into 1^{1}/$_{2}$-inch chunks

Simply the Best Beef Stew

Step 6

Step 9

1 Preheat the oven to 325°F.

2 In a small bowl, combine 1 1/2 teaspoons of the salt and the pepper. Sprinkle and pat this mixture on the meat.

3 Heat a Dutch oven over medium-high heat for 1 to 2 minutes.

4 Add the oil to the pot and heat up for about 20 seconds.

5 Add 1/3 of the meat to the pot, leaving space around each piece.

6 Cook the meat, using tongs to turn the meat until all sides of the meat are deep brown in color, about 8 minutes. Remove and place in a large bowl.

7 Repeat steps 5 and 6 with the remaining meat. Add more oil to the pot if necessary.

8 Reduce the heat to medium.

9 Add the onions and the remaining 1/2 teaspoon of salt to the pot. Cook until the onions are softened, frequently scraping the bottom of the pot with a wooden spoon, about 5 minutes.

Tip

Can I still make this recipe if I don't have a Dutch oven?

Yes. You can use a 5 1/2 or 6 quart sauté pan and a large ovenproof casserole dish instead. Use the sauté pan for steps 3 to 13 below. Then turn off the heat under the pan and use tongs and a perforated skimmer to carefully place all the ingredients into the ovenproof casserole dish. Pour the sauce overtop, cover and place the casserole dish in the oven to finish cooking.

Nutrition Facts Per Serving	
Calories	684
Calories from Fat	266
Total Fat	30 g
Saturated Fat	10 g
Monounsaturated Fat	14 g
Polyunsaturated Fat	2 g
Cholesterol	116 mg
Sodium	932 mg
Total Carbohydrates	57 g
Dietary Fiber	7 g
Sugars	8 g
Protein	42 g

10 Add the carrots and cook, stirring occasionally, for about 3 minutes.

11 Add the tomato paste and stir continuously for 1 minute.

12 Pour the beer (or red wine) into the pot. Increase the heat to medium-high and cook, stirring continuously, until half of the liquid has evaporated, about 2 minutes.

13 Add the broth, lentils, potatoes, meat and meat juices. Stir to combine and bring to a boil.

14 Once the mixture is boiling, place a cover on the pot and then place the pot in the oven.

15 Bake until the meat is tender when pierced with a fork, about 2 1/2 to 3 hours.

16 Remove from the oven and allow the stew to sit, uncovered, for 10 minutes. Gently stir before serving.

The Perfect Steak

There are only a few simple rules you need to follow to grill a perfect steak every time.

First, the more tender the meat you start out with, the better your grilled steak will be. Tender cuts that are good for grilling include rib eye, strip, T-bone and sirloin steaks. For best results, your steaks should be about 1 inch thick, cut into serving-sized portions and completely patted dry before going on the grill.

Second, the grill must be preheated and very hot before you begin. The grill needs a high heat to properly sear the outside of the meat and keep the juices inside.

Finally, you need to give the steak time to rest before serving, so the juices can flow throughout the meat, making every bite juicy and delicious.

The cooking times suggested below are approximate, and can vary according to the thickness of the meat, the weather and the type of grill you are using.

The Perfect Steak

Step 4

Step 5

1 Preheat your grill on high for 15 minutes.

2 Use paper towels to pat both sides of the steak completely dry. Then sprinkle and pat kosher or sea salt and freshly ground black pepper onto both sides of the steak.

3 To prevent the steak from sticking to your grill grates, use grill tongs to dip a bunched up paper towel into a bowl of vegetable oil and then rub the oil on the grates.

4 Use grill tongs to place the steak on the grill at a 45-degree angle.

5 Cook for 2 minutes. Then rotate the steak 90 degrees to create a crosshatch pattern on the steak.

6 For a medium-rare steak, continue to cook the first side for 2 to 3 minutes more.

- For rare, continue cooking for 1 to 2 minutes more. For medium, continue cooking for 3 to 4 minutes more. For well-done, continue cooking for 4 to 5 minutes more.

Tip

How do you like your steak?

- Rare
  A rare steak is red on the inside and warm throughout.

- Medium-Rare
  A medium-rare steak is reddish pink in the center and very warm throughout.

- Medium
  A medium steak is pink in the center and hot throughout.

- Well-Done
  A well-done steak is gray-brown and hot throughout.

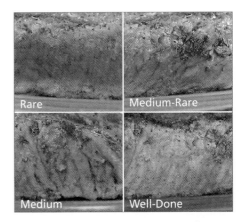

7 When the steak is cooked on the first side, use grill tongs to turn the steak over.

8 For medium rare, cook the steak for 3 to 4 minutes on the second side.

- For rare, cook the steak for 2 to 3 minutes on the second side. For medium, cook for 4 to 5 minutes. For well-done, cook for 6 to 7 minutes.

9 When the steak is cooked, use clean grill tongs to remove the steak from the grill and place the steak on a clean plate.

10 Allow the steak to rest on the plate for 3 to 4 minutes. Resting allows the juices to be redistributed throughout the steak so the entire steak is juicy.

11 Serve the steak with the crosshatch pattern facing up.

Traditional Pork Schnitzel

This traditional pork dish features breaded and shallow-fried boneless pork loin chops. You will need to pound the pork chops to get them to a uniform thickness and ensure fast, even cooking. For information on pounding meat, see page 74. This recipe also works well with pounded boneless chicken breasts.

Makes 4 servings

INGREDIENTS

1/3 cup all-purpose flour

2 eggs

1 1/2 cups Italian style bread crumbs

4 boneless pork loin chops, pounded less than 1/4 inch thick

1/2 cup canola or safflower oil, plus more if needed

Traditional Pork Schnitzel

Flour   Eggs & water   Bread crumbs

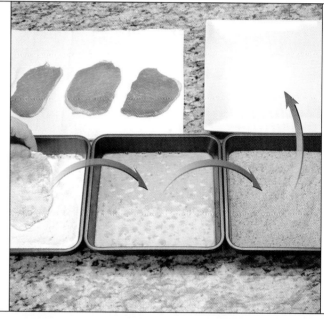

1 Set up three baking pans or pie plates in a row.

2 Place the flour in the first pan.

3 In the second pan, combine the eggs with 4 teaspoons of water. Beat together very lightly with a fork.

4 Place the bread crumbs in the third pan.

5 Pat the pounded pork loin chops dry using paper towels.

6 Place one pork loin chop in the flour. Coat well on both sides and shake off the excess flour.

7 Place the pork in the egg mixture. Coat well on both sides and allow the excess egg to drip off.

8 Place the pork in the bread crumbs. Cover the top surface with bread crumbs and press down. Shake off any excess bread crumbs.

9 Place the chop on a large plate.

10 Repeat steps 6 to 9 for the rest of the pork.

Tip

There are bread crumbs accumulating on the bottom of the skillet. What should I do?

If you notice that loose bread crumbs are beginning to gather at the bottom of the skillet after you remove the pork, it is time to change the oil in the skillet. Before frying the next batch of pork, discard the used oil, use a paper towel to carefully wipe out all the loose crumbs from the skillet, add 1/2 cup of fresh oil, heat for 30 seconds and then continue preparing the schnitzel.

Nutrition Facts Per Serving	
Calories	591
Calories from Fat	297
Total Fat	33 g
Saturated Fat	7 g
Monounsaturated Fat	16 g
Polyunsaturated Fat	6 g
Cholesterol	167 mg
Sodium	735 mg
Total Carbohydrates	38 g
Dietary Fiber	2 g
Sugars	2 g
Protein	33 g

Step 13

Step 15

11 Heat a large skillet over medium-high heat for 1 to 2 minutes.

12 Add 1/2 cup of oil to thoroughly cover the bottom surface of the skillet. Wait 20 seconds.

13 Carefully place a breaded pork loin chop into the oil.

14 Fry on the first side until golden brown, using tongs to move the pork around occasionally, 1 1/2 to 2 minutes.

15 Using tongs, carefully turn the chop over. Fry on the second side until golden brown, about 1 1/2 to 2 minutes.

16 Place the pork loin chop on a baking sheet lined with paper towels to drain any excess oil.

17 Repeat steps 13 to 16 for the remaining pork. Add more oil to the pan if necessary to ensure that the bottom surface of the skillet is thoroughly covered in oil.

- Try serving this dish with mixed salad greens tossed with the Citrus dressing shown on page 137.

One-Pan Pork Chops & Rice

One-Pan Pork Chops & Rice is a meal in a pan. You can choose to use regular stewed tomatoes or a flavored version, such as Italian or Mexican. To add some pizzazz to this dish, try adding 1 teaspoon of dried thyme leaves, 1 sliced bell pepper, 3/4 cup of mushroom halves and 1/3 cup of pitted black olives along with the onions in this recipe.

Makes 4 servings

INGREDIENTS

2 teaspoons seasoned salt

1/4 teaspoon pepper

2 tablespoons extra virgin olive oil (plus more if needed)

4 pork chops, bone-in

1 cup long-grain converted rice, uncooked

1 1/2 cups low-sodium chicken or beef broth

1 medium onion, halved and sliced 1/4-inch thick

1 can (14.5 ounces) stewed tomatoes

One-Pan Pork Chops & Rice

1 Preheat the oven to 350°F.

2 Lightly grease the inside of a 9x13 baking pan with oil.

3 In a small bowl, combine the seasoned salt and pepper. Sprinkle and pat this mixture onto both sides of the pork chops.

4 Heat a large skillet over medium-high heat for 1 to 2 minutes.

5 Add 2 tablespoons of olive oil to the skillet and allow to heat up for about 20 seconds.

6 Add two of the pork chops to the skillet, leaving space around each piece.

7 Cook the pork chops, turning once with tongs, until both sides are browned, about 5 minutes.

8 Remove the pork chops and place on a plate.

9 Repeat steps 6 to 8 with the two remaining pork chops. Add more oil to the pan if necessary.

10 Spread the rice evenly over the bottom of the oiled baking pan.

Can I make this dish with chicken instead of pork?

For an easy chicken dish, prepare this recipe using 4 bone-in chicken breasts or legs. Scatter the onions, stewed tomatoes and 2 cloves of minced garlic over the rice before placing the browned chicken on top. Then add in the broth and sprinkle the juice of half a lemon, 1 teaspoon of dried oregano leaves and some freshly grated black pepper over the surface. Cook until the rice has absorbed most of the liquid and the chicken is no longer pink when cut near the bone, about 1 hour.

Nutrition Facts Per Serving	
Calories	514
Calories from Fat	196
Total Fat	22 g
Saturated Fat	6 g
Monounsaturated Fat	12 g
Polyunsaturated Fat	2 g
Cholesterol	76 mg
Sodium	1245 mg
Total Carbohydrates	49 g
Dietary Fiber	1 g
Sugars	7 g
Protein	29 g

Step 12

Steps 13 & 14

11 Layer the pork chops on top of the rice, overlapping only if necessary.

12 Pour the chicken (or beef) broth over the pork chops, making sure there are some spaces between the chops to allow the broth to seep into the rice below.

13 Scatter the onion on top of the pork chops and rice.

14 Spoon the stewed tomatoes, including the liquid, evenly over the surface of each pork chop.

15 Cover the baking pan tightly with aluminum foil and bake until the rice has absorbed most of the broth and the pork has no more than a hint of pink when cut with a knife, about 1 hour to 1 hour and 15 minutes.

16 Remove the pork chops from the baking pan. Stir the rice.

- Serve the pork chops with the rice.

Cranberry Glazed Pork Tenderloin

This pork recipe combines the distinctive flavor of cranberry sauce with other flavorful ingredients, including juniper berries, gin and red wine vinegar. After browning the pork tenderloin on the stovetop, you transfer the entire skillet to the oven to finish cooking. If your skillet has a plastic handle, you can easily ovenproof the handle by wrapping it with 2 or 3 layers of aluminum foil.

Makes 4 to 6 servings

INGREDIENTS

1 can (14 to 16 ounces) jellied cranberry sauce
1/2 cup tomato juice
2 tablespoons red wine vinegar
2 cloves garlic, minced
2 tablespoons grainy or plain Dijon mustard
2 tablespoons extra virgin olive oil, plus 2 tablespoons
2 teaspoons dried juniper berries, lightly crushed (optional)
1 1/2 teaspoons salt and 1/4 teaspoon pepper
1/2 cup dry gin or low-sodium chicken broth
2 pork tenderloins (3/4 pound to 1 pound each), patted dry

Cranberry Glazed Pork Tenderloin

1 In a medium bowl, add the cranberry sauce. Mash well using a potato masher.

2 Add the tomato juice, vinegar, garlic, mustard, 2 tablespoons of oil, juniper berries (if using), salt and pepper to the bowl. Stir well with a spoon to combine.

3 Place 1 cup of the mixture in a small stainless steel or glass bowl. Cover with plastic wrap and refrigerate.

4 Add 1/2 cup of gin (or chicken broth) to the remaining cranberry mixture and stir well to combine. Set aside.

5 Place the pork in a large glass dish.

6 Pour the marinade with the gin over the pork. Turn the pork over, rubbing the marinade over all surfaces with your hands.

7 Cover and let the pork sit in the marinade in the refrigerator for at least 4 hours, or overnight, turning once or twice.

8 When ready to cook, preheat the oven to 375°F.

9 Remove the pork from the marinade. Using paper towels, blot the pork until it is totally dry.

Tip

How can I make this delicious sauce even tastier?

You can deglaze the pan to make the sauce even more flavorful. Simply add 1/2 cup of gin or low-sodium chicken broth to the large skillet that the pork was in and cook over medium-high heat, scraping the bottom of the pan with a wooden spoon until only half of the liquid remains. Then add the liquid instead of the boiling water in step 17 below to the cranberry mixture and stir well. For more information on deglazing, see page 117.

Nutrition Facts Per Serving	
Calories	462
Calories from Fat	147
Total Fat	16 g
Saturated Fat	3 g
Monounsaturated Fat	11 g
Polyunsaturated Fat	2 g
Cholesterol	88 mg
Sodium	911 mg
Total Carbohydrates	37 g
Dietary Fiber	2 g
Sugars	24 g
Protein	29 g

10 Heat a large ovenproof skillet (not non-stick) at medium-high heat for 1 to 2 minutes.

11 Add 2 tablespoons of oil to the skillet and swirl to coat the surface of the skillet.

12 Place the tenderloins in the skillet and brown well on two sides, about 4 minutes.

13 Place the skillet in the oven and cook until only a hint of pink remains in the center of the pork, about 15 to 20 minutes.

14 While the pork is cooking, place the refrigerated marinade into a small saucepan.

15 Over medium heat, bring the marinade to a simmer, stirring often. Simmer for 10 minutes. Then turn the heat to low and stir occasionally.

16 When the pork is finished cooking, remove the skillet from the oven. Using tongs, place the pork on a cutting board to rest for 10 minutes.

17 Add 1/4 cup of boiling water to the small saucepan and stir.

18 Slice the pork. Strain the sauce through a medium fine mesh strainer and serve with the pork.

Paprika Mushroom Chicken

Here is a twist on the Hungarian classic, chicken paprikash. This version uses a common staple in most homes—canned tomato soup. Don't let the number of onions in the recipe scare you. They actually melt away during cooking to create a luscious sauce. To cut down on the fat and calories without compromising the flavor, remove the skin from the chicken pieces before you begin.

Makes 4 servings

INGREDIENTS

1/4 cup all-purpose flour
1 teaspoon seasoned salt
4 chicken breasts or legs, bone-in
2 tablespoons extra virgin olive oil, plus more if needed
3 medium onions, diced into 1/4-inch pieces
1 teaspoon salt and 1/4 teaspoon pepper
1/2 pound white or brown mushrooms, sliced
1 can (10.75 ounces) condensed tomato soup, plus 1 can water
1 tablespoon paprika
2 bay leaves

Paprika Mushroom Chicken

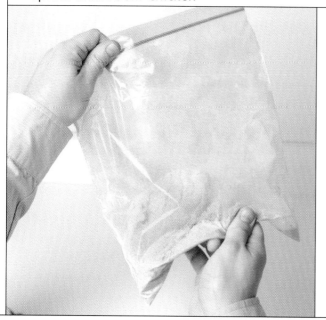

1 Place the flour and seasoned salt in a large resealable bag. Shake well to combine.

2 Add one or two of the chicken pieces to the flour mixture. Shake the bag to coat the chicken with the mixture.

3 Remove the chicken from the bag, shaking off any excess flour, and place the chicken on a large plate.

4 Repeat steps 2 and 3 with the remaining chicken pieces.

5 Heat a large sauté pan over medium-high heat for 1 to 2 minutes.

6 Add the oil to the pan and allow to heat up for about 20 seconds.

7 Add two chicken pieces to the pan, with the skin side down.

8 Cook the chicken, turning once using tongs, until both sides are a deep golden brown, about 6 minutes.

9 Remove the chicken and place on a large plate.

10 Repeat steps 7 to 9 with the two remaining chicken pieces. Add more oil to the pan if necessary.

Tip

I don't like mushrooms. Can I change the sauce for this dish?

You can easily vary the sauce you use in this dish. Perform steps 1 to 11 below. Then instead of performing steps 12 and 13, simply add your favorite jar of pasta sauce, a store-bought simmer sauce, or get creative and design your own signature sauce! You can then perform steps 14 to 17 as indicated to finish cooking the dish.

Nutrition Facts Per Serving	
Calories	319
Calories from Fat	79
Total Fat	9 g
Saturated Fat	1 g
Monounsaturated Fat	6 g
Polyunsaturated Fat	1 g
Cholesterol	68 mg
Sodium	1465 mg
Total Carbohydrates	28 g
Dietary Fiber	3 g
Sugars	11 g
Protein	31 g

Step 11

Step 14

11 Reduce the heat to medium. In the same pan, add the onions and 1/2 teaspoon of the salt. Stir often until softened, about 5 minutes.

12 Increase the heat to medium high. Add the mushrooms and stir occasionally until lightly browned, about 5 minutes.

13 Add the tomato soup, water, paprika, remaining 1/2 teaspoon of salt, pepper and bay leaves. Stir well to combine.

14 Return the chicken to the pan. Coat the chicken with the sauce and bring to a boil.

15 Reduce the heat and simmer, allowing the mixture to gently bubble. Cover the sauté pan with a lid.

16 Let the mixture simmer, stirring occasionally, until the chicken is tender and the juices run clear when the chicken is pierced with a paring knife, about 40 minutes.

17 Turn off the heat, remove the lid and let the pan sit for 10 minutes. Remove the bay leaves.

18 Try serving this dish with cooked egg noodles or with the mashed potatoes shown on page 152.

Asian Chicken Stir-Fry

This Asian Chicken Stir-Fry combines crisp vegetables, tender chicken strips and fabulous Asian flavors. Instead of purchasing chicken strips, which can be expensive, simply buy 1 pound of boneless chicken breasts and cut them into 1/4-inch strips. The secret to a great stir-fry is to have all of the ingredients ready before you start cooking. There won't be any time for cutting vegetables once your sauté pan is hot.

Makes 4 servings

INGREDIENTS

1/4 cup oyster sauce
2 tablespoons soy sauce
2 garlic cloves, minced
3 tablespoons extra virgin olive oil
1 pound chicken stir-fry strips
1 medium onion, cut into 1/2-inch slices
1/2 pound fresh snow peas, strings removed
1 medium zucchini, cut into sticks
1 red pepper, cut into strips
1 can (14 ounces) baby corn, drained and rinsed (optional)

Asian Chicken Stir-Fry

1 In a small bowl, combine the oyster sauce, soy sauce and garlic using a whisk. Set aside.

2 Heat a large sauté pan over medium-high heat for 1 to 2 minutes.

3 Add 2 tablespoons of the oil to the pan and heat up for 20 seconds.

4 Add the chicken strips to the pan and cook, tossing continuously with two wooden spoons, until no longer pink, about 3 to 4 minutes. Place into a bowl and set aside.

5 Add the remaining 1 tablespoon of oil to the pan.

6 Add the onion and snow peas to the pan and cook, tossing continuously for 2 minutes.

Tip

Can I use other vegetables in my stir-fry?

You can change the vegetables in this stir-fry recipe to suit your tastes. Some vegetables, such as cauliflower, broccoli and green beans, benefit from being dropped into boiling water until they are almost cooked, a process known as parboiling, and then placed in an ice bath (see page 104) before being added to your stir-fry. Advance parboiling of your vegetables helps to cut down on your stir-frying time.

Nutrition Facts Per Serving	
Calories	385
Calories from Fat	122
Total Fat	14 g
Saturated Fat	2 g
Monounsaturated Fat	9 g
Polyunsaturated Fat	2 g
Cholesterol	66 mg
Sodium	866 mg
Total Carbohydrates	37 g
Dietary Fiber	6 g
Sugars	9 g
Protein	33 g

7 Add the zucchini and red pepper to the pan and cook, tossing continuously for 2 minutes.

8 Add the baby corn (if using), chicken and oyster sauce mixture to the pan and cook, stirring continuously for about 1 minute, until the sauce and other ingredients are well combined.

• Serve over rice or Asian noodles.

Asian Seafood Stir-Fry

• You can use shrimp or scallops instead of chicken in this recipe. Simply substitute 1 pound of raw shrimp or scallops for the chicken in step 4 and cook for two minutes. Then add the shrimp or scallops back into the pan in step 8, along with the other ingredients.

Pesto Chicken Roll-Ups

The flavors of mozzarella cheese and pesto come together beautifully in these intriguing Pesto Chicken Roll-Ups. Pounding the chicken breasts flattens the chicken for easier rolling. For information on pounding meat, see page 74. For an extra crispy coating, try using 1 1/2 tablespoons of Japanese panko crumbs instead of 1 tablespoon of bread crumbs for each chicken breast.

Makes 4 servings

INGREDIENTS

1 teaspoon salt and 1/4 teaspoon pepper

4 boneless chicken breasts, pounded 1/4-inch thick

4 tablespoons basil pesto or sun-dried tomato pesto sauce

1/2 cup shredded mozzarella cheese blend or mozzarella

4 teaspoons extra virgin olive oil

2 tablespoons Dijon mustard

4 tablespoons dry bread crumbs

Pesto Chicken Roll-Ups

Step 5

Step 6

Step 8

1 Preheat the oven to 375°F.

2 Cover the bottom of a baking sheet with parchment paper.

3 In a small bowl, combine the salt and pepper. Sprinkle and pat this mixture onto both sides of the chicken.

4 On a large plate, place one chicken breast smooth side down, with the narrowest end closest to you.

5 Place 1 tablespoon of pesto onto the center of the breast. Spread the pesto evenly over the breast using a pastry brush.

6 Sprinkle 2 tablespoons of shredded cheese over the pesto, keeping a 1/2 inch cheese-free border around the breast.

7 Starting at the end closest to you, carefully roll up the chicken breast.

8 Using 4 toothpicks, secure the end of the breast. Place the breast, toothpick side down, on the prepared baking sheet.

9 Repeat steps 4 to 8 with the remaining chicken breasts.

Tip

Can I prepare this dish in advance?

Preparing this dish in advance will get you out of the kitchen and give you more time to mingle at your next dinner party. Perform steps 3 to 9 below up to 24 hours before you plan to serve this dish. Place the prepared chicken onto a platter, cover it with plastic wrap and place it in the refrigerator. About 45 minutes before you are ready to serve the roll-ups place the chicken on a prepared baking sheet and complete the recipe.

Nutrition Facts Per Serving	
Calories	272
Calories from Fat	114
Total Fat	13 g
Saturated Fat	4 g
Monounsaturated Fat	6 g
Polyunsaturated Fat	2 g
Cholesterol	81 mg
Sodium	952 mg
Total Carbohydrates	6 g
Dietary Fiber	1 g
Sugars	1 g
Protein	32 g

Step 12

10 Slowly pour 1 teaspoon of oil over each breast. Use a pastry brush to coat the top and the sides of each breast.

11 Place 1 1/2 teaspoons of Dijon mustard on top of each breast. Use a pastry brush to coat the top and sides of each breast.

12 Carefully sprinkle 1 tablespoon of bread crumbs over the top and along the sides of each breast, using your fingers to pat the crumbs onto the sides.

13 Bake until the chicken is firm and no longer pink inside, approximately 20 to 25 minutes.

14 Remove the chicken from the oven and let stand for 5 minutes before removing the toothpicks.

15 Using a chef's knife, slice each breast 1/2-inch to 1-inch thick on the diagonal before serving.

Tangy Glazed Chicken

Whether it's prepared for a weekday meal or for your next dinner party, everyone will think you spent hours on this delicious chicken dish. This Tangy Glazed Chicken has a bit of an Asian flavor, with a combination of sweet, sour and savory ingredients that blend together to form a delicious glaze and sauce.

Makes 4 servings

INGREDIENTS

2 teaspoons garlic powder

1 teaspoon salt and ¼ teaspoon pepper

1 large onion, minced

⅔ cup apricot jam or orange marmalade

2 teaspoons yellow mustard

½ teaspoon ground ginger or grated fresh ginger

1 tablespoon soy sauce

1 tablespoon cider vinegar or rice vinegar

4 chicken breasts or legs, bone-in

Tangy Glazed Chicken

Step 2

Steps 3 & 4

1 Preheat the oven to 350°F.

2 Lightly coat the inside of a 9x13 baking pan with oil.

3 In a small bowl, mix together the garlic powder, salt and pepper with a whisk. Set aside.

4 In a medium bowl, mix together the onion, apricot jam (or orange marmalade), mustard, ginger, soy sauce and vinegar. Set aside.

5 Place the chicken pieces skin side up in a single layer on the baking pan.

6 Sprinkle the chicken with the garlic powder mixture.

Tip *How can I give the recipe a little more kick?*

This recipe calls for a small amount of ginger—just enough to contribute to the flavor of the dish without being very noticeable. If you are a big fan of ginger, try doubling the amount in the recipe to 1 teaspoon to give this dish a little extra ginger kick.

Nutrition Facts Per Serving	
Calories	383
Calories from Fat	100
Total Fat	11 g
Saturated Fat	2 g
Monounsaturated Fat	5 g
Polyunsaturated Fat	3 g
Cholesterol	82 mg
Sodium	1009 mg
Total Carbohydrates	41 g
Dietary Fiber	1 g
Sugars	35 g
Protein	30 g

7 Spoon the onion mixture evenly over the chicken pieces.

8 Bake the chicken for 45 minutes and remove the pan from the oven.

9 Using a serving spoon, spoon the pan juices over the chicken pieces.

10 Bake until the chicken is browned and the juices run clear when the chicken is pierced with a paring knife, about 15 to 25 minutes.

• Try serving this dish with rice.

Roasted Chicken & Vegetables

This roast chicken recipe creates delicious pan juices that you can spoon over the chicken as it cooks to create browned and flavorful moist skin. After the chicken is cooked, you can put the pan juices in a bowl to serve with the chicken as a gravy. This recipe also allows you to cook the vegetables alongside the chicken. It's truly a meal in one pan.

Makes 6 servings

INGREDIENTS

1 tablespoon garlic powder
1 tablespoon onion powder
1 1/2 teaspoons dry mustard
1/2 teaspoon dried rosemary or Italian seasoning
1 teaspoon salt and 1/4 teaspoon pepper
1 large onion, halved and sliced 1/4-inch thick
4 medium carrots, halved lengthwise and cut into thirds
4 stalks celery, cut into thirds
2 tablespoons extra virgin olive oil
1 whole chicken (3 to 3 1/2 pounds)

Roasted Chicken & Vegetables

1. Preheat the oven to 400°F.

2. Keep a kettle of boiling water available during the roasting of the chicken.

3. In a small bowl, combine the garlic powder, onion powder, dry mustard, rosemary (or Italian seasoning), salt and pepper. Stir with a whisk until blended and set aside.

4. In the center of a roasting pan, place the onion slices, carrots and celery.

5. Sprinkle the vegetables with oil and 1 1/2 teaspoons of the seasoning mix.

6. Toss the vegetables with your hands to coat evenly. Arrange the vegetables evenly over the surface of the pan.

7. Using paper towels, pat dry the outside and the cavity of the chicken.

8. Sprinkle 1 1/2 teaspoons of the seasoning mix into the chicken's cavity.

9. Sprinkle and pat the remaining seasoning mixture over the entire surface of the chicken.

Tip

How can I get a crispier skin on my roast chicken?

If you prefer a more crispy-skinned roast chicken but still want the ready-to-serve pan juices, do not spoon the pan juices over the chicken in steps 13 and 15 below. You should still, however, add the boiling water to the pan as instructed in these steps.

Nutrition Facts Per Serving	
Calories	575
Calories from Fat	352
Total Fat	39 g
Saturated Fat	11 g
Monounsaturated Fat	18 g
Polyunsaturated Fat	8 g
Cholesterol	170 mg
Sodium	651 mg
Total Carbohydrates	11 g
Dietary Fiber	3 g
Sugars	4 g
Protein	43 g

Step 10

Step 12

10 Place the chicken in the center of the roasting pan.

11 Cook for 30 minutes. Remove the pan from the oven.

12 Pour 1 1/2 cups of boiling water over the vegetables in the pan. Then cook for 20 minutes.

13 Remove the pan from the oven. Spoon the pan juices over the chicken and vegetables. Then add 1 cup of boiling water to the pan and cook for 20 more minutes.

14 Remove the pan from the oven.

15 Spoon the pan juices over the chicken and vegetables. Add 1/2 cup of boiling water only if the pan juices seem to be drying up.

16 Cook until the chicken is golden brown and the juices run clear when a paring knife is inserted between the thigh and breast, about 10 to 20 minutes.

17 Place the chicken on a cutting board and allow it to rest for 10 minutes.

18 Serve the chicken with the vegetables and the pan juices.

Shrimp Scampi

If you are a fan of seafood, Shrimp Scampi is the dish for you. The delectable combination of shrimp, garlic and butter is irresistible. Feel free to use either fresh or previously frozen, raw shrimp in this recipe. Before using the shrimp, rinse the shrimp in cold water, drain well and pat them dry.

Makes 4 servings

INGREDIENTS

1/4 cup all-purpose flour
1/4 teaspoon salt and 1/4 teaspoon pepper
1 pound large raw shrimp, peeled and deveined, patted dry
2 tablespoons extra virgin olive oil
1 shallot, minced
3 cloves garlic, minced
1/2 cup bottled clam juice
1 tablespoon fresh lemon juice
1/4 cup (1/2 stick) unsalted butter, cut into 1/2-inch cubes
2 tablespoons finely chopped Italian parsley

Shrimp Scampi

Step 1

Step 3

1 In a medium bowl, mix together the flour, salt and pepper with a whisk.

2 Add the shrimp to the bowl. Mix well with your hands to coat the shrimp with the flour mixture.

3 Place the floured shrimp in a medium, fine mesh strainer held over the sink. Shake the strainer to remove any excess flour from the shrimp. Set aside.

4 Heat a large skillet or sauté pan over medium heat for 1 to 2 minutes.

5 Add the oil to the skillet and heat for about 20 seconds.

6 Add the shrimp, minced shallot and garlic to the skillet and cook, stirring continuously, for 1 minute.

Tips

Can I use other types of seafood in this dish?

For variety, try this dish with scallops. Simply substitute 1 pound of raw scallops for the shrimp. Make sure you rinse and pat the scallops dry before using them in the dish.

Can I spice up my Shrimp Scampi?

To add a bit of spice to this dish, try stirring in a peeled and seeded diced tomato and 1/8 teaspoon (or more) of red pepper flakes in step 7 below. To peel and seed a tomato, see page 78.

Nutrition Facts Per Serving	
Calories	315
Calories from Fat	178
Total Fat	20 g
Saturated Fat	8 g
Monounsaturated Fat	8 g
Polyunsaturated Fat	2 g
Cholesterol	203 mg
Sodium	382 mg
Total Carbohydrates	8 g
Dietary Fiber	0 g
Sugars	0 g
Protein	24 g

7 Add the clam juice, lemon juice and butter to the skillet.

8 Cook, stirring occasionally, until the shrimp are just firm and opaque and the sauce has thickened slightly, about 2 to 3 minutes.

9 Turn off the heat and stir the chopped parsley into the mixture.

• Serve with pasta or rice.

Pan-Fried Tilapia

Pan-Fried Tilapia is a tasty way to get more of the health benefits of fish into your diet. For a healthy and hearty salad, try tossing your favorite mixed greens with a citrus or fat-free tomato dressing (see page 136) and top the salad with these delectable tilapia fillets.

Makes 4 servings

INGREDIENTS

2 tablespoons all-purpose flour
1/2 teaspoon garlic powder
1/4 teaspoon dry mustard
1/4 teaspoon curry powder
1/2 teaspoon salt and 1/8 teaspoon pepper
4 tilapia or red snapper fillets, patted dry
1/4 cup extra virgin olive oil

Pan-Fried Tilapia

1 In a shallow pan, mix together the flour, garlic powder, dry mustard, curry powder, salt and pepper with a whisk.

2 Place one fillet in the flour mixture and coat well on both sides. Shake off any excess flour mixture and place the fillet on a large plate.

3 Repeat step 2 with the remaining fillets.

4 Heat a large skillet over medium-high heat for 1 to 2 minutes.

5 Add the oil to the skillet and heat for about 20 seconds.

6 Carefully place two fillets in the skillet.

Tip *Can I make my own tartar sauce at home?*

Try this recipe for an easy homemade tartar sauce. Combine 1/3 cup of low-fat mayonnaise, 1 1/2 tablespoons of sweet relish, 1 tablespoon of minced onion, 1 1/2 teaspoons of fresh lemon juice, 1/8 teaspoon of salt and a pinch of pepper. Stir well to blend and enjoy.

Nutrition Facts Per Serving	
Calories	361
Calories from Fat	153
Total Fat	17 g
Saturated Fat	3 g
Monounsaturated Fat	11 g
Polyunsaturated Fat	2 g
Cholesterol	81 mg
Sodium	441 mg
Total Carbohydrates	3 g
Dietary Fiber	0 g
Sugars	0 g
Protein	45 g

7 Cook, turning once, until the fish is golden brown on each side and the flesh is firm when touched, about 4 minutes.

8 Place the fillets on a platter and cover loosely with aluminum foil.

9 Repeat steps 6 to 8 with the two remaining fillets.

• Serve the fillets with tartar sauce. To make homemade tartar sauce, see the top of this page.

• For some great sandwiches, cut four large crusty rolls in half and spread with tartar sauce. Place one pan-fried tilapia fillet on each roll, add some sliced tomato and lettuce and you have a terrific lunch or light supper.

Roasted Glazed Salmon

This salmon dish creatively combines the sweetness of honey with the gentle bite of Dijon mustard and ancho chili powder to tantalize your taste buds. When cooked properly, salmon has a delicate, almost velvety texture. To achieve this texture, it is best to cook salmon until it is not quite done in the center.

Makes 4 servings

INGREDIENTS

4 salmon fillets (about 7 ounces each), patted dry

1/4 cup low-fat mayonnaise

2 teaspoons water

1 1/2 teaspoons liquid honey

1 teaspoon Dijon mustard

1 teaspoon ancho chili powder

1/4 teaspoon garlic powder

1/8 teaspoon salt and 1/8 teaspoon pepper

2 green onions, sliced 1/8-inch wide

Roasted Glazed Salmon

1 Preheat the oven to 450°F.

2 Cover the bottom of a baking sheet with parchment paper.

3 Place the salmon fillets on the prepared baking sheet, skin side down.

4 In a small bowl, whisk together the mayonnaise, water, honey, Dijon mustard, ancho chili powder, garlic powder, salt and pepper to prepare the glaze.

Tip

Can I serve this salmon dish cold?

This dish is also great served cold. You can prepare the salmon as instructed and then refrigerate it for up to 24 hours before serving. When cold, this dish is a fantastic addition to any buffet table. Don't forget to make some extra glaze and serve it as a sauce on the side.

Nutrition Facts Per Serving	
Calories	608
Calories from Fat	251
Total Fat	28 g
Saturated Fat	4 g
Monounsaturated Fat	9 g
Polyunsaturated Fat	12 g
Cholesterol	221 mg
Sodium	287 mg
Total Carbohydrates	5 g
Dietary Fiber	0 g
Sugars	2 g
Protein	79 g

5 Using a pastry brush, apply one-quarter of the prepared glaze evenly over the top and sides of each salmon fillet.

6 Place the baking sheet in the oven.

7 Cook until the very center of the thickest part of one of the fillets is still slightly underdone when cut into with a paring knife, about 15 minutes.

- The very center of the salmon should look slightly darker than the surrounding area and still be a bit glossy and translucent.

8 Sprinkle the sliced green onions evenly over the fillets.

- Try serving this dish with mixed salad greens tossed with a citrus dressing (see page 137).

Thai Coconut Curry Fish

This Thai-inspired dish blends the flavors of coconut milk with shallots, garlic and Thai curry paste to create a delicious coconut curry sauce.

Before serving your Thai Coconut Curry Fish, try sprinkling with some coarsely chopped cilantro and serving with wedges of lime for squeezing over the fish.

Makes 4 servings

INGREDIENTS

1 1/2 pounds haddock or halibut fillets, skin removed
1 tablespoon extra virgin olive oil
2 shallots, halved and thinly sliced
2 garlic cloves, thinly sliced
1 can (14 ounces) light coconut milk
1/2 cup low-sodium vegetable or chicken broth
2 tablespoons Asian fish sauce
1 tablespoon liquid honey
1 teaspoon Thai green or red curry paste
3/4 cup frozen peas (do not thaw)

Thai Coconut Curry Fish

Step 5

Step 6

1 Rinse the haddock (or halibut) fillets under cold running water. Cut into 1-inch chunks and set aside.

2 Heat a large sauté pan or skillet over medium heat for 1 to 2 minutes.

3 Add the oil to the pan and heat for about 20 seconds.

4 Add the shallots to the pan and cook, stirring often, for 2 minutes.

5 Add the garlic to the pan and cook, stirring often, for 1 minute.

6 Add the coconut milk, vegetable (or chicken) broth, fish sauce, honey and curry paste to the pan. Stir well to combine.

7 Still at medium heat, bring the mixture to a simmer, allowing the mixture to gently bubble.

8 Cook, stirring often, for about 5 minutes.

Tip

How can I change the spice level of this dish?

You can change the spice level of this dish by decreasing or increasing the amount of Thai curry paste you use. If you prefer milder foods, use only 1/2 teaspoon of curry paste. You can add more, if needed, while the sauce is cooking. If you enjoy spicier foods, use more than 1 teaspoon of Thai curry paste.

Nutrition Facts Per Serving	
Calories	324
Calories from Fat	98
Total Fat	11 g
Saturated Fat	6 g
Monounsaturated Fat	3 g
Polyunsaturated Fat	1 g
Cholesterol	97 mg
Sodium	954 mg
Total Carbohydrates	14 g
Dietary Fiber	2 g
Sugars	8 g
Protein	35 g

9 Add the frozen peas and bring the mixture back to a simmer.

10 Place the fish chunks into the mixture and stir.

11 Increase the heat to medium high and bring back to a simmer, gently tossing occasionally using two wooden spoons.

12 Cook until the fish is firm and opaque, about 4 to 5 minutes, adjusting the heat as needed to maintain the simmer.

• Serve with white jasmine or brown rice.

Thai Coconut Curry Chicken

• You can use chicken instead of fish in this recipe. Simply substitute 1 1/2 pounds of boneless chicken breasts or thighs cut into 1-inch chunks for the fish in step 10. Cook until the chicken is no longer pink inside, about 4 to 6 minutes.

Ultimate Chocolate Chip Cookies

Rich and decadent, these are the Ultimate Chocolate Chip Cookies. If you would like to alter the chocolate taste, try replacing the semi-sweet chocolate chips with milk chocolate, white chocolate or even butterscotch chips.

Makes approximately 48 cookies

INGREDIENTS

2 1/4 cups all-purpose flour

1 teaspoon baking soda

1/2 teaspoon salt

2 eggs

1 cup (2 sticks) unsalted butter, cut into 1/2-inch slices

3/4 cup granulated sugar

2/3 cup packed brown sugar

2 teaspoons pure vanilla extract

2 cups semi-sweet chocolate chips

Ultimate Chocolate Chip Cookies

Step 6

Step 7

1 Preheat the oven to 375°F.

2 Cover the bottom of two baking sheets with parchment paper.

3 In a medium bowl, mix together the flour, baking soda and salt with a whisk. Set aside.

4 Break the eggs and place into a small bowl. Set aside.

5 In a small bowl, melt the butter in a microwave for about 1 minute, stirring after 30 seconds.

6 Pour the melted butter into a large bowl and then add the granulated sugar, brown sugar and vanilla to the bowl.

7 Using an electric hand mixer, beat the ingredients together at medium speed for about 2 minutes.

8 Add the eggs to the bowl and beat at medium speed until thoroughly combined.

Tip

What should I do if my cookies won't fit on two baking sheets?

If the cookie dough does not fit on two baking sheets, reuse the first baking sheet and parchment paper after the first batch of baked cookies has been placed on the cooling racks. Allow the first baking sheet to cool before using for another batch of cookies.

Nutrition Facts Per Cookie	
Calories	132
Calories from Fat	60
Total Fat	7 g
Saturated Fat	4 g
Monounsaturated Fat	1 g
Polyunsaturated Fat	0 g
Cholesterol	18 mg
Sodium	55 mg
Total Carbohydrates	17 g
Dietary Fiber	0 g
Sugars	12 g
Protein	1 g

9 Add in one quarter of the flour mixture, beating at a low speed until thoroughly combined.

10 Repeat step 9 for each of the remaining three quarters of the flour mixture.

11 Scrape off any remaining dough from the hand mixer blades and add to the mixture.

12 Stir in the chocolate chips with a rubber spatula.

13 Drop one heaping teaspoon of dough at a time, spaced 1 1/2 inches apart, onto the baking sheets.

14 Bake each sheet separately until the cookie tops are golden brown and their edges are lightly browned, about 9 to 12 minutes.

15 Let the cookies cool on the baking sheet for about 3 minutes.

16 Using a spatula, place the cookies on cooling racks to cool completely.

Double Chocolate Brownies

These brownies are so rich and gooey, they don't need any frosting. For the best results when melting the chocolate, you need a medium heatproof glass or stainless steel bowl that fits securely over a large saucepan. The bottom of the bowl must be several inches above the bottom of the saucepan to ensure the bowl does not touch the simmering water in the saucepan.

Makes 16 servings

INGREDIENTS

4 ounces unsweetened chocolate (4 squares), cut in quarters

3/4 cup semi-sweet chocolate chips

1/2 cup (1 stick) unsalted butter, cut into small chunks

2 teaspoons finely ground espresso or dark roast coffee (optional)

3 eggs

3/4 cup granulated sugar

2 teaspoons pure vanilla extract

1/2 cup all-purpose flour

1/2 teaspoon baking powder

1/4 teaspoon salt

Double Chocolate Brownies

1 Preheat the oven to 350°F.

2 Use a pastry brush to lightly coat a 9x9 or 8x8 baking pan with vegetable shortening or melted butter.

3 Fill a large saucepan with 1 inch of water. Place the saucepan on the stove and bring to a simmer so the water is gently bubbling.

4 Place the unsweetened chocolate, chocolate chips and butter in a medium heatproof glass or stainless steel bowl.

5 Place the bowl over the saucepan, making sure that the bottom of the bowl does not touch the water.

6 Using an oven mitt to hold the bowl, stir occasionally with a heat-proof spatula until the chocolate and butter are melted, about 5 minutes.

7 Remove the bowl from the saucepan and place on a heatproof surface. Stir the espresso (if using) into the chocolate mixture and set aside.

Tip

Can I add even more flavor to these brownies?

These brownies are decadent just as they are, but if you want to add some extra flavor and texture, try stirring an additional 1 cup of semi-sweet chocolate chips or 1 1/2 cups of pecan or walnut halves into the batter just before you pour the batter into the prepared baking pan in step 11 below.

Nutrition Facts Per Serving	
Calories	188
Calories from Fat	113
Total Fat	13 g
Saturated Fat	8 g
Monounsaturated Fat	4 g
Polyunsaturated Fat	1 g
Cholesterol	50 mg
Sodium	52 mg
Total Carbohydrates	20 g
Dietary Fiber	2 g
Sugars	14 g
Protein	3 g

8 Add the eggs and sugar to a medium bowl and whisk until the mixture is light and fluffy, about 2 to 3 minutes. Then whisk in the vanilla until blended.

9 Slowly whisk the chocolate mixture into the egg mixture. Whisk continuously until blended.

10 In a small bowl, whisk together the flour, baking powder and salt. Add the mixture to the chocolate and egg mixture and blend using a rubber spatula.

11 Pour the batter into the prepared baking pan, using a spatula to evenly spread the batter.

12 Bake until a toothpick inserted within one inch of the edge of the pan comes out dry, about 20 to 25 minutes. At the same time, a toothpick inserted in the center should come out with traces of melted chocolate and some moist crumbs.

13 Remove the baking pan from the oven and allow to cool completely in the pan on a cooling rack before cutting into squares.

Cheesecake Squares

Cheesecake is a popular dessert. Most people, however, don't realize that making cheesecake can be quite simple. This recipe is extremely versatile—the squares are great on their own or topped with berries or chocolate sauce. Once your cheesecake has cooled, place plastic wrap directly onto the top of the cheesecake to keep it from drying out.

Makes 24 squares

INGREDIENTS
3 eggs
1 1/2 cups graham cracker crumbs
3/4 cup granulated sugar
1/2 cup (1 stick) melted unsalted butter
1 pound (2 packages) reduced-fat cream cheese, softened
1 cup part-skim ricotta cheese
1 cup low-fat sour cream
1/4 teaspoon salt
1 tablespoon fresh lemon juice
2 teaspoons pure vanilla extract

Cheesecake Squares

Step 5

Steps 7 & 8

1 Preheat the oven to 350°F.

2 Use a pastry brush to lightly coat the bottom and sides of a 9x13 baking pan with vegetable shortening or coat with baking spray.

3 Break the eggs into a small bowl. Set aside.

4 In a medium bowl, combine the graham cracker crumbs, 2 tablespoons of the sugar and the melted butter. Stir with a fork to blend well.

5 Using your fingers, spread the graham cracker mixture evenly over the bottom of the prepared pan. Pat the crumb mixture down firmly with the back of a spoon.

6 In a large bowl, add the cream cheese and remaining sugar.

7 Using a hand mixer at low speed, beat the cheese and sugar until smooth.

8 Add the eggs, ricotta cheese, sour cream, salt, lemon juice and vanilla to the bowl. Beat the ingredients at a low speed until thoroughly combined.

Tips

How do I soften cream cheese?

To soften cream cheese, simply remove it from its original packaging, wrap in plastic wrap and keep at room temperature for 1 to 2 hours.

Why do cheesecakes sometimes crack?

If over-baked, cheesecakes have a tendency to crack while they cool. Be sure to check on your cheesecake regularly during those last few minutes of baking to avoid this problem. If your cheesecake does end up cracking, just place some berries over the crack when serving and no one will notice.

Nutrition Facts Per Square	
Calories	161
Calories from Fat	91
Total Fat	10 g
Saturated Fat	6 g
Monounsaturated Fat	3 g
Polyunsaturated Fat	1 g
Cholesterol	51 mg
Sodium	137 mg
Total Carbohydrates	13 g
Dietary Fiber	0 g
Sugars	8 g
Protein	5 g

9 Pour the cream cheese mixture evenly over the graham cracker crust in the pan, using a rubber spatula to remove all of the cheesecake batter from the bowl.

10 Spread the cheesecake batter evenly in the pan using the rubber spatula.

11 Bake until a 3-inch section in the center of the cheesecake still looks slightly liquidy when the pan is jiggled, but the area outside of the center is firm, about 22 to 27 minutes.

Note: The cheesecake will appear to be under-baked, but it is not.

12 Place on a cooling rack for 15 minutes. Then place in the refrigerator, uncovered, to chill for at least 2 hours before serving. Cut into squares to serve.

Rise & Shine Cranberry Muffins

Rise & Shine Cranberry Muffins combine the tartness of cranberries with the sweetness of orange juice to create a delicious way to start your day. These muffins are also very healthy, providing antioxidants and heart-healthy fat. Be sure to keep the cranberries frozen until you need them. Once the cranberries begin to thaw, their bright red color will seep into the batter, discoloring your muffins.

Makes 12 muffins

INGREDIENTS

2 cups all-purpose flour
1 cup packed brown sugar
1 1/2 teaspoons baking soda
1/2 teaspoon salt
3/4 cup quick oats (not instant)
2 eggs
3/4 cup orange juice
3/4 cup 1% milk
1/2 cup olive oil (not extra virgin) or vegetable oil
1 cup frozen unsweetened cranberries (do not thaw)

Rise & Shine Cranberry Muffins

Step 3

Step 5

1 Preheat the oven to 375°F.

2 Use a pastry brush to lightly coat the cups of a muffin pan with melted butter or vegetable shortening.

• You can use paper muffin baking cups instead of coating the cups with butter or vegetable shortening.

3 In a large bowl, add the flour, brown sugar, baking soda and salt. Mix well with a whisk.

4 Add the oats to the flour mixture. With the whisk, stir until well combined. Set aside.

5 In a medium bowl, add the eggs, orange juice, milk and oil. Stir with a whisk until well combined. Set aside.

Variations!

Variety is the spice of life. You can change the entire flavor of these muffins by simply playing around with different frozen fruits. Give frozen raspberries, blueberries or mixed berries a try.

Can I freeze my muffins?

These muffins freeze nicely when individually wrapped in plastic wrap and placed in a resealable freezer bag. When you're ready for a nice, fresh muffin, simply remove one from the freezer, unwrap it, pop it in the microwave for about a minute and enjoy!

Nutrition Facts Per Muffin	
Calories	276
Calories from Fat	100
Total Fat	11 g
Saturated Fat	2 g
Monounsaturated Fat	7 g
Polyunsaturated Fat	1 g
Cholesterol	32 mg
Sodium	280 mg
Total Carbohydrates	40 g
Dietary Fiber	1 g
Sugars	21 g
Protein	4 g

6 Add the frozen cranberries to the flour and oat mixture.

7 Pour the liquid mixture into the large bowl.

8 Using a rubber spatula, stir the batter to combine. Do not overmix the batter or the muffins will have a tough texture.

9 Using a 1/3-cup measuring cup, scoop the batter into the muffin cups, filling each cup completely.

10 Bake until the tops of the muffins are firm to the touch, about 20 to 24 minutes.

11 Remove the muffin pan from the oven and let the muffins cool for 5 minutes.

12 Carefully lift each muffin out of the pan and place on a cooling rack until completely cooled.

Crowd-Pleasing Cornbread

A southern classic, this Crowd-Pleasing Cornbread is sure to be a winner. If you don't have a 9x5x3 loaf pan, you can also use an 8.5x4.5x2.5 loaf pan. To help maintain the freshness of the cornbread, wrap the cooled loaf in plastic wrap or place it in a sealed plastic bag. The leftovers won't last long though!

Makes 8 servings

INGREDIENTS

1 cup yellow cornmeal
1 cup all-purpose flour, plus extra to coat the pan
1 tablespoon granulated sugar
1 teaspoon baking soda
1/2 teaspoon salt and 1/4 teaspoon pepper
2 eggs
1 can (14 ounces) creamed corn
1/2 cup buttermilk (shake carton before using)
1/4 cup olive oil (not extra virgin)
1/2 cup frozen corn kernels, thawed and patted dry

Crowd-Pleasing Cornbread

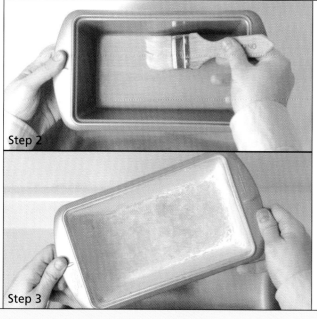

Step 2

Step 3

1 Preheat the oven to 400°F.

2 Use a pastry brush to lightly coat the bottom and sides of a 9x5x3 loaf pan with vegetable shortening or melted butter.

3 Holding the pan over the sink, sprinkle some flour inside the pan. Turn the pan to coat the bottom and all four sides with flour. Then shake out the excess flour.

4 In a large bowl, mix together the cornmeal, flour, sugar, baking soda, salt and pepper with a whisk. Set aside.

5 In a medium bowl, mix together the eggs, creamed corn, buttermilk and oil with a whisk.

6 Add the corn kernels and the liquid ingredients to the dry ingredients. Stir with a rubber spatula until just blended.

Are there any ways I can vary this recipe?

To add some zip to your cornbread, try adding 1/4 cup of drained and diced canned green chilies to the liquid ingredients. For cheesy cornbread, add 1/2 cup of grated cheddar or Monterey Jack cheese to the dry cornmeal mixture.

Nutrition Facts Per Serving	
Calories	266
Calories from Fat	101
Total Fat	11 g
Saturated Fat	2 g
Monounsaturated Fat	6 g
Polyunsaturated Fat	1 g
Cholesterol	48 mg
Sodium	432 mg
Total Carbohydrates	40 g
Dietary Fiber	3 g
Sugars	6 g
Protein	7 g

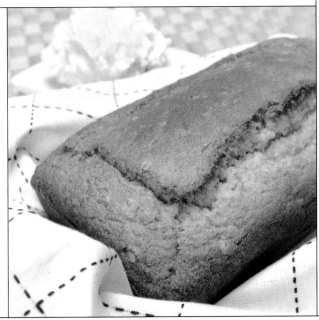

7 Pour the mixture into the prepared pan. Tap the bottom of the pan gently on the countertop to remove any air bubbles.

8 Bake until the top of the cornbread is well browned with no signs of wetness and a toothpick inserted into the center comes out clean, about 45 to 50 minutes.

9 Place the cornbread on a cooling rack for 15 minutes.

10 Carefully run a knife between the cornbread and the sides of the pan.

11 Remove the cornbread from the pan and let cool on a cooling rack for at least 15 minutes before slicing.

• Try serving this cornbread with the Vegetable Bean Soup on page 130 for a light lunch. This cornbread is also delicious served with the Come Back for More Chili on page 172.

Lemony Pound Cake

This Lemony Pound Cake is moist and buttery, with a sublime lemon flavor. A stand mixer is best for mixing this cake, but you can also get great results with a hand mixer—simply beat the mixture for a bit longer than specified below. Don't forget to scrape down the sides of the bowl to incorporate all the ingredients when beating.

Makes 10 servings

INGREDIENTS

1²/3 cups cake flour
1 teaspoon baking powder
¹/2 teaspoon salt
1 tablespoon finely grated lemon zest
4 eggs
1 cup (2 sticks) unsalted butter, softened
1¹/4 cups granulated sugar
¹/4 cup fresh lemon juice
2 teaspoons pure vanilla extract

Lemony Pound Cake

1 Preheat the oven to 325°F.

2 Spray the bottom and sides of a 9x5x3 loaf pan with baking spray.

3 Place a medium fine mesh strainer over a medium bowl and add the flour, baking powder and salt.

4 Shake the strainer to allow the flour mixture to pass through to the bowl. Use a spoon to press the ingredients through if necessary.

5 Add the lemon zest to the bowl and stir with a whisk.

6 In a small bowl, gently beat the eggs with a whisk. Set aside.

7 Place the butter into the bowl of a stand mixer.

8 Beat the butter at medium speed until it is creamy and light in color, about 3 minutes.

9 Continue to beat the butter and slowly add the sugar. Continue to beat until the mixture is light and fluffy, about 5 to 6 minutes.

Tip

Why do I have to beat the butter with the sugar for so long?

Beating butter and sugar together is called creaming and is vital to ensure that a large volume of air bubbles is incorporated into the butter. Of all the steps in a cake recipe like this one, beating the butter together with the sugar is the most important. For perfect results, never beat these ingredients for less than the time specified in the recipe.

Nutrition Facts Per Serving	
Calories	371
Calories from Fat	178
Total Fat	20 g
Saturated Fat	12 g
Monounsaturated Fat	5 g
Polyunsaturated Fat	1 g
Cholesterol	123 mg
Sodium	193 mg
Total Carbohydrates	44 g
Dietary Fiber	0 g
Sugars	25 g
Protein	4 g

10 Continue beating as you add one third of the beaten eggs. Beat to combine, about 30 seconds.

11 Repeat step 10 for each of the remaining two thirds of the eggs. Beat until the mixture is airy, about 2 minutes.

12 Add half of the flour mixture and blend well with a rubber spatula.

13 Add the lemon juice and blend well. Then add the remaining flour mixture and blend well.

14 Add the vanilla and stir until blended.

15 Using a rubber spatula, spread the batter in the prepared pan, smoothing the top with the back of a spoon.

16 Bake until the cake is a deep golden brown and a toothpick inserted into the center comes out clean, about 65 to 70 minutes.

17 Remove the cake from the oven and place the pan on a cooling rack. Allow to cool for 15 minutes.

18 Remove the cake from the pan and let cool completely on the cooling rack.

References

As you are cooking and baking, you are bound to come across terms that you are wondering about. This section features a glossary that explains many of those unfamiliar terms. If you ever come across metric measurements when cooking, this section also includes a handy metric conversion chart.

13 Reference & Measurements
Glossary
Metric Conversion Chart

Glossary

A

Al dente
An Italian phrase meaning "to the tooth," usually used to describe pasta that is cooked until tender, but still firm.

B

Baste
Spoon, brush or drizzle sauce, pan drippings or other liquid over food during cooking to keep the food moist and to add flavor.

Batter
An uncooked, semi-liquid mixture, which you can scoop up with a spoon (for muffins) or pour (for pancakes). A batter usually contains flour, liquids and one or more ingredients, such as baking soda, which makes the batter rise when cooked. Batters can also be used to coat the surface of food before frying.

Beat
Mix ingredients rapidly until the ingredients are well blended. Beating is often used to add air to an ingredient, such as egg whites or heavy cream. Beating is also known as whipping.

Blanch
Plunge vegetables or fruit in boiling water for a brief period of time to loosen their skin or enhance and preserve their color and flavor.

Blend
Mix two or more ingredients together with a spoon, whisk, spatula, electric mixer or other kitchen utensil until combined.

Braise
Cook meat, poultry or vegetables covered, in a small amount of liquid at low heat for a long period of time. The slow cooking tenderizes and adds flavor to food.

Broil
Cook food directly below a heat source, typically under an oven's broiling element. Broiling is a dry heat method of cooking which is suitable for chicken, fish, seafood and tender cuts of meat.

Brown
Cook food at a high temperature, usually on top of the stove, causing the outside surfaces of the food to turn brown. Browning meat, poultry and fish creates a flavorful crust and helps seal in a food's juices. Browning food is also known as searing food.

C

Caramelize

Foods caramelize when their natural sugars come to the surface during heating and cause browning. For example, root vegetables brown and sweeten when roasted, and seared meats, fish and poultry develop browned crusts with intense flavors. Desserts such as crème brulee, are caramelized from above, using a broiler or blow torch. Caramelize also means to heat sugar slowly on the stove until it turns into a golden-brown, caramel-flavored syrup.

Chiffonade

Cut the leaves of herbs or leafy vegetables, such as basil or lettuce, into thin strips. In French, chiffonade means "made of rags."

Chop

Cut food into pieces using a knife or food processor. Chopped food can range in size from finely chopped (minced) to coarsely chopped.

Coat

Coat the surface of food by covering the food in flour, breadcrumbs, marinades, dressings or other dry or wet ingredients.

Core

Remove the center of a fruit or vegetable, such as an apple or bell pepper.

Cream

Beat a fat, most often butter, until it is light in color and fluffy. Recipes for buttery baked goods often call for creaming a mixture of butter and sugar.

Crisp-tender

Describes the texture of vegetables which are cooked until they are still slightly firm but no longer raw, and can be pierced easily with a paring knife.

Cube

Cut food into square pieces 1/2 inch or larger, using a knife.

D

Deglaze

After cooking meat, poultry, fish or vegetables, dissolve the browned bits stuck to the bottom of the pan by adding a liquid such as wine, beer or broth and stirring over heat. The resulting mixture can be used as the flavor base for a sauce or gravy.

Degrease

Remove the fat that forms on the surface of soup, broth or sauces, using a spoon. Degreasing can also be done by chilling the liquid and then removing the fat on the liquid's surface. Degreasing is also known as skimming off the fat.

De-vein
Remove the dark intestinal vein running from the head to the tail of a shrimp. De-veining shrimp is a common technique used when preparing shrimp for cooking.

Dice
Cut food into cubed or squared pieces, about 1/4 inch to 3/4 inch in size, using a knife.

Dough
An uncooked mixture that you can scoop up with a spoon (for cookies), roll (for pie crust) or knead (for bread). Dough usually contains flour, liquid and sometimes an ingredient such as yeast, which makes the dough rise when cooked. Unlike batter, dough is too stiff to pour.

Dredge
Coat the surface of food by dipping the food in flour, breadcrumbs or other dry ingredients.

Drizzle
Pour liquid, such as melted butter or salad dressing, in a thin stream over food.

F

Flake
Break off small pieces of food, usually with a fork. Flaking is often done to determine if fish is properly cooked.

Fold
Combine a light airy mixture, such as beaten egg whites, into a heavier mixture, such as a cake batter, using a gentle stirring and lifting motion.

Fry
Cook or sauté food in oil over high temperatures. Deep-fried foods are cooked by submerging them in hot oil. Shallow-fried and pan-fried foods are only partially submerged in hot oil.

G

Garnish
A decorative, edible addition, such as parsley or croutons, to a finished dish. A garnish enhances the appearance of a dish and should complement the flavor of a dish.

Glaze
Coat the surface of baked goods with a liquid mixture, such as melted chocolate or melted jam. Also, to coat meat, poultry or fish with a liquid mixture prior to roasting or grilling.

Grate

Rub food, such as cheese, vegetables or the peel of citrus fruits, against the small, sharp holes of a grater to produce smaller food pieces. Grating is also known as shredding.

Grease

Coat the surface of a pan, such as a muffin pan, with a thin layer of fat, such as shortening or melted butter, to prevent the food from sticking to the pan. Alternately, a baking spray or cooking spray may be used.

H

Hull

Remove the stem and leaves from a strawberry or other berry to prepare it for eating.

I

Ice bath

A large bowl filled with water and ice into which you place hot food to rapidly chill the food and stop the cooking process. Ice baths preserve the color and texture of foods just after they have been boiled, parboiled, blanched or steamed.

J

Juice

Extract the juice from a fruit.

Julienne

Cut food into thin, matchstick-sized strips. Julienne-cut foods are often used as garnishes or salad toppings.

K

Knead

Work dough using a pressing, folding and turning motion until the dough is elastic and has a smooth texture. You can knead dough with your hands, a bread machine, a food processor or an electric mixer with a dough hook.

M

Marinate

Soak food such as meat, poultry, fish or vegetables in a seasoned, liquid mixture for a period of time to add flavor to food before cooking. The seasoned, liquid mixture used to marinate foods is called a marinade.

Mince

Cut food into very fine pieces using a knife or food processor.

Mirepoix

A mixture of cut-up onions or leeks, carrots and celery, which is used as the flavor base for stocks, sauces, soups and stews.

Glossary

P

Parboil
Cook food, such as carrots or broccoli, in boiling water until the food is almost done.

Pinch
A small amount of a dry ingredient, such as salt or pepper, which can be held between the tips of the thumb and index finger. A pinch is equal to approximately 1/16 teaspoon.

Poach
Cook foods, such as eggs and fish, in barely simmering liquid, which is just below the boiling point.

Pound
Flatten pieces of meat, such as chicken breasts, into an even thickness, using the flat side of a meat tenderizer. Pounding meat often speeds up the cooking time and can increase the tenderness of meat.

Purée
Mash or blend food until the food has a smooth and uniform consistency, using a blender or food processor or by forcing the food through a sieve.

R

Reduce
Boil liquid, such as stock or sauce, to evaporate some of the liquid in order to thicken the liquid and intensify its flavor.

Refresh
See Shock.

Roast
Cook food, such as meat, poultry, fish or vegetables, uncovered in the oven, usually without adding any liquid. Roasted foods generally have a browned exterior and moist interior.

S

Sauté
Cook food quickly in a small amount of fat, typically oil or butter, over very high heat in a skillet or sauté pan. In French, sauté means "to jump," which describes how food is constantly tossed in a pan when sautéed.

Score
Make shallow cuts in the surface of food, such as meat, fish and bread. Scoring is done to decorate food as well as help food absorb flavors and moisture from mixtures such as marinades.

Sear
See Brown.

Season
Add flavor to foods in the form of salt, pepper, herbs, spices or other ingredients, to improve their taste.

Shock

Plunge hot food, usually vegetables, in ice water to rapidly chill the food and stop the cooking process. Shocking food is also known as refreshing food.

Shred

See Grate.

Sift

Pass dry ingredients, such as flour or sugar, through a fine mesh sifter or strainer to create a powdery consistency. Sifting ingredients removes any large pieces and makes the ingredients airier.

Simmer

Cook liquids on the stove or in the oven at a temperature just below the boiling point. Tiny bubbles will rise slowly and break gently at the liquid's surface. Foods are often cooked in a simmering liquid.

Skim

See Degrease.

Soften

Leave cold food, such as butter or cream cheese, at room temperature until it becomes soft.

Steam

Cook food over a small amount of boiling or simmering water in a covered pan so the steam rising from the water cooks the food.

Stew

Brown less tender cuts of meat or vegetables in oil, then cover with a flavored liquid and slowly cook at low heat for a long period of time. The slow moist heat method of cooking tenderizes and adds flavor to the food. Stewed foods are usually served along with their thickened cooking liquid.

Sweat

Cook food, typically onion, garlic or other vegetables, in a small amount of oil or butter over low heat until the food is slightly softened, without browning.

W

Whip

See Beat.

Whisk

A hand-held wire kitchen tool used to beat ingredients such as eggs and cream. Also describes the act of beating ingredients with a whisk.

Z

Zest

The colored, outer skin of lemons, oranges and other citrus fruits. Also, using a citrus zester or paring knife to remove the colored, outer skin of a citrus fruit in thin strips while leaving the bitter white pith behind.

Metric Conversion Chart

VOLUME

U.S. Units	Metric
1/4 teaspoon	1 ml
1/2 teaspoon	2 ml
1 teaspoon	5 ml
1 tablespoon	15 ml
1/4 cup	50 ml
1/3 cup	75 ml
1/2 cup	125 ml
2/3 cup	150 ml
3/4 cup	175 ml
1 cup	250 ml
1 quart	1 liter
1 1/2 quarts	1.5 liters
2 quarts	2 liters
2 1/2 quarts	2.5 liters
3 quarts	3 liters
4 quarts	4 liters

TEMPERATURES

Fahrenheit	Celsius
32°	0°
212°	100°
250°	120°
275°	140°
300°	150°
325°	160°
350°	180°
375°	190°
400°	200°
425°	220°
450°	230°
475°	240°
500°	260°

WEIGHT

U.S. Units	Metric
1 ounce	30 grams
2 ounces	55 grams
3 ounces	85 grams
4 ounces (1/4 pound)	115 grams
8 ounces (1/2 pound)	225 grams
16 ounces (1 pound)	455 grams

MEASUREMENTS

Inches	Centimeters
1/8	0.3 (3 millimeters)
1/4	0.6 (6 millimeters)
1/2	1.3
3/4	1.9
1	2.5
1 1/2	3.8
2	5

Note

The recipes in this book were not developed or tested using metric measurements. If you convert the recipes to metric, keep in mind that the quality of some recipes may be affected. When cooking, be sure to use a consistent system of measurement throughout a recipe.

Index

Index

Index

Index

Did you like this book? MARAN ILLUSTRATED™ offers books on the most popular computer topics, using the same easy-to-use format of this book. We always say that if you like one of our books, you'll love the rest of our books too!

Here's a list of some of our best-selling computer titles:

Guided Tour Series - 240 pages, Full Color

MARAN ILLUSTRATED's Guided Tour series features a friendly disk character that walks you through each task step by step. The full-color screen shots are larger than in any of our other series and are accompanied by clear, concise instructions.

	ISBN-10	ISBN-13	Price
MARAN ILLUSTRATED™ Computers Guided Tour	1-59200-880-1	978-1-59200-880-3	$24.99 US/$33.95 CDN
MARAN ILLUSTRATED™ Windows XP Guided Tour	1-59200-886-0	978-1-59200-886-5	$24.99 US/$33.95 CDN

MARAN ILLUSTRATED™ Series - 320 pages, Full Color

This series covers 30% more content than our Guided Tour series. Learn new software fast using our step-by-step approach and easy-to-understand text. Learning programs has never been this easy!

	ISBN-10	ISBN-13	Price
MARAN ILLUSTRATED™ Access 2003	1-59200-872-0	978-1-59200-872-8	$24.99 US/$33.95 CDN
MARAN ILLUSTRATED™ Computers	1-59200-874-7	978-1-59200-874-2	$24.99 US/$33.95 CDN
MARAN ILLUSTRATED™ Excel 2003	1-59200-876-3	978-1-59200-876-6	$24.99 US/$33.95 CDN
MARAN ILLUSTRATED™ Mac OS® X v.10.4 Tiger™	1-59200-878-X	978-1-59200-878-0	$24.99 US/$33.95 CDN
MARAN ILLUSTRATED™ Office 2003	1-59200-890-9	978-1-59200-890-2	$29.99 US/$39.95 CDN
MARAN ILLUSTRATED™ Windows XP	1-59200-870-4	978-1-59200-870-4	$24.99 US/$33.95 CDN

101 Hot Tips Series - 240 pages, Full Color

Progress beyond the basics with MARAN ILLUSTRATED's 101 Hot Tips series. This series features 101 of the coolest shortcuts, tricks and tips that will help you work faster and easier.

	ISBN-10	ISBN-13	Price
MARAN ILLUSTRATED™ Windows XP 101 Hot Tips	1-59200-882-8	978-1-59200-882-7	$19.99 US/$26.95 CDN

 PIANO

MARAN ILLUSTRATED™ **Piano**
is an information-packed resource
for people who want to learn to
play the piano, as well as current
musicians looking to hone their skills.
Combining full-color photographs and
easy-to-follow instructions, this guide
covers everything from the basics
of piano playing to more advanced
techniques. Not only does MARAN
ILLUSTRATED™ Piano show you how
to read music, play scales and chords
and improvise while playing with
other musicians, it also provides
you with helpful information for
purchasing and caring for your piano.

ISBN-10: 1-59200-864-X
ISBN-13: 978-1-59200-864-3
Price: $24.99 US; $33.95 CDN
Page count: 304

illustrated DOG TRAINING

MARAN ILLUSTRATED™ **Dog Training**
is an excellent guide for both current
dog owners and people considering
making a dog part of their family.
Using clear, step-by-step instructions
accompanied by over 400 full-color
photographs, MARAN ILLUSTRATED™
Dog Training is perfect for any visual
learner who prefers seeing what to do
rather than reading lengthy explanations.

Beginning with insights into popular
dog breeds and puppy development,
this book emphasizes positive training
methods to guide you through
socializing, housetraining and teaching
your dog many commands. You will
also learn how to work with problem
behaviors, such as destructive chewing.

ISBN-10: 1-59200-858-5
ISBN-13: 978-1-59200-858-2
Price: $19.99 US; $26.95 CDN
Page count: 256

MARAN ILLUSTRATED™ Knitting & Crocheting contains a wealth of information about these two increasingly popular crafts. Whether you are just starting out or you are an experienced knitter or crocheter interested in picking up new tips and techniques, this information-packed resource will take you from the basics, such as how to hold the knitting needles or crochet hook, to more advanced skills, such as how to add decorative touches to your projects. The easy-to-follow information is communicated through clear, step-by-step instructions and accompanied by over 600 full-color photographs—perfect for any visual learner.

ISBN-10: 1-59200-862-3
ISBN-13: 978-1-59200-862-9
Price: $24.99 US; $33.95 CDN
Page count: 304

MARAN ILLUSTRATED™ Yoga provides a wealth of simplified, easy-to-follow information about the increasingly popular practice of Yoga. This easy-to-use guide is a must for visual learners who prefer to see and do without having to read lengthy explanations.

Using clear, step-by-step instructions accompanied by over 500 full-color photographs, this book includes all the information you need to get started with yoga or to enhance your technique if you have already made yoga a part of your life. MARAN ILLUSTRATED™ Yoga shows you how to safely and effectively perform a variety of yoga poses at various skill levels, how to breathe more efficiently and much more.

ISBN-10: 1-59200-868-2
ISBN-13: 978-1-59200-868-1
Price: $24.99 US; $33.95 CDN
Page count: 320

MARAN ILLUSTRATED™ Weight Training is an information-packed guide that covers all the basics of weight training, as well as more advanced techniques and exercises.

MARAN ILLUSTRATED™ Weight Training contains more than 500 full-color photographs of exercises for every major muscle group, along with clear, step-by-step instructions for performing the exercises. Useful tips provide additional information and advice to help enhance your weight training experience.

MARAN ILLUSTRATED™ Weight Training provides all the information you need to start weight training or to refresh your technique if you have been weight training for some time.

ISBN-10: 1-59200-866-6
ISBN-13: 978-1-59200-866-7
Price: $24.99 US; $33.95 CDN
Page count: 320

MARAN ILLUSTRATED™ Poker is an essential resource that covers all aspects of the most popular poker games, including Texas Hold'em, Omaha and Seven-Card Stud. You will also find valuable information on playing in tournaments, bluffing, feeling at home in a casino and even playing poker online.

This information-packed guide includes hundreds of detailed, full-color illustrations accompanying the step-by-step instructions that walk you through each topic. MARAN ILLUSTRATED™ Poker is a must-have for anyone who prefers a visual approach to learning rather than simply reading explanations.

Whether you are a novice getting ready to join in a friend's home game or you are an experienced poker player looking to hone your tournament skills, MARAN ILLUSTRATED™ Poker provides all the poker information you need.

ISBN-10: 1-59200-946-8
ISBN-13: 978-1-59200-946-6
Price: $19.99 US; $26.95 CD
Page count: 240

MARAN ILLUSTRATED™ Guitar is an excellent resource for people who want to learn to play the guitar, as well as for current musicians who want to fine tune their technique. This full-color guide includes over 500 photographs, accompanied by step-by-step instructions that teach you the basics of playing the guitar and reading music, as well as advanced guitar techniques. You will also learn what to look for when purchasing a guitar or accessories, how to maintain and repair your guitar, and much more.

Whether you want to learn to strum your favorite tunes or play professionally, MARAN ILLUSTRATED™ Guitar provides all the information you need to become a proficient guitarist.

ISBN-10: 1-59200-860-7
ISBN-13: 978-1-59200-860-5
Price: $24.99 US; $33.95 CDN
Page count: 320

MARAN ILLUSTRATED™ Cooking Basics is an information-packed resource that covers all the basics of cooking. Novices and experienced cooks alike will find useful information about setting up and stocking your kitchen as well as food preparation and cooking techniques. With over 500 full-color photographs illustrating the easy-to-follow, step-by-step instructions, this book is a must-have for anyone who prefers seeing what to do rather than reading long explanations.

MARAN ILLUSTRATED™ Cooking Basics also provides over 40 recipes from starters, salads and side-dishes to main course dishes and baked goods. Each recipe uses only 10 ingredients or less, and is complete with nutritional information and tips covering tasty variations and commonly asked questions.

ISBN-10: 1-59863-234-5
ISBN-13: 978-1-59863-234-7
Price: $19.99 US; $26.95 CDN
Page count: 240

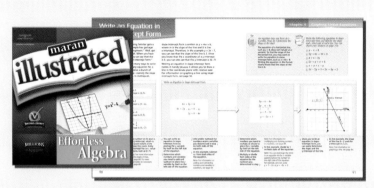
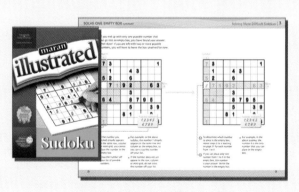

MARAN ILLUSTRATED™ Bartending
is the perfect book for those who want to impress their guests with cocktails that are both eye-catching and delicious. This indispensable guide explains everything you need to know about bartending in the most simple and easy-to-follow terms. MARAN ILLUSTRATED™ Bartending has recipes, step-by-step instructions and over 400 full-color photographs of all the hottest martinis, shooters, blended drinks and warmers. This guide also includes a section on wine, beer and alcohol-free cocktails as well as information on all of the tools, liquor and other supplies you will need to start creating drinks right away!

ISBN-10: 1-59200-944-1
ISBN-13: 978-1-59200-944-2
Price: $19.99 US; $26.95 CDN
Page count: 256